From
Fiction
to
Film:

Ambrose Bierce's
"AN OCCURRENCE AT
OWL CREEK BRIDGE"

The Dickenson Literature and Film Series:

From Fiction to Film: Conrad Aiken's
"Silent Snow, Secret Snow"

From Fiction to Film: Ambrose Bierce's
"An Occurrence at Owl Creek Bridge"

Forthcoming:

From Fiction to Film: D. H. Lawrence's
"The Rocking-Horse Winner"

The Dickenson Literature and Film Series

From Fiction to Film:

Ambrose Bierce's
"AN OCCURRENCE AT OWL CREEK BRIDGE"

Gerald R. Barrett
University of Delaware

Thomas L. Erskine
Salisbury State College

Dickenson Publishing Company, Inc.
Encino, California
Belmont, California

To our parents.

ISBN-0-8221-0083-5
Library of Congress Catalog Card Number: 72-87316
Printed in the United States of America
Printing (last digit): 9 8 7 6 5 4 3 2 1

Contents

Contents

Preface

From Fiction to Film is a new approach to the teaching of short stories, films, and the art of adaptation. By concentrating on the problems involved in transforming one medium of art to another, the student, we believe, will learn a great deal about both fiction and film.

The book begins with an introduction that presents the general problem of transforming fiction to film; it then provides the student with an opportunity to put his knowledge to work. A short story is reprinted and followed by relevant critical articles of varying approach and depth, so that the student can read the literary work and consider it from a number of diverse perspectives before he sees either or both films and reads the critical essays devoted to them. (The existence of two film versions of the Ambrose Bierce story offers an added dimension.) In order to facilitate comparisons between the short story and the films, we have printed shot analyses of the finished movies. In this way, the student will not have to rely on memory, but can refer to the printed text of the films' sound and visuals. Critical essays on the films follow the shot analyses. Finally, the book contains suggested topics for themes and term papers. In fact, it may be used as a casebook since it includes the original pagination of the reprinted criticism.

We hope that this book will be of value to teachers both of literature and of film and that those students who use it will gain new insights into both art forms and develop an appreciation of the creative problems as well as the artistic rewards of adaptations.

Our special thanks go to Raymond Rohauer, copyright owner of the film, "The Bridge" ("The Spy"), for his kind help and his permission to create a shot analysis of the film. Stills from "The Bridge" ("The Spy") have been supplied by courtesy of Raymond Rohauer, copyright owner. We also wish to thank Professors Herbert Bergman of Michigan State, Fred Marcus of California State College, Los Angeles, and Tom Sobchack of University of Utah for their helpful criticism and thoughtful suggestions and Mr. Peter Massardo as well as the Instructional Resources Center of the University of Delaware for technical assistance.

Gerald R. Barrett
University of Delaware
Thomas L. Erskine
Salisbury, Maryland

INTRODUCTION

GERALD R. BARRETT

From Fiction
to Film

Most of us, at one time or another, have heard the following comments about a film based on a novel or a short story: "I liked the novel better." "What a lousy film; I'll never read the book." "Boy, did they ruin a fine short story." "This film did the novel justice." Viewers making such statements too often assume that the differences between the art of prose fiction and the art of film are slight, if, indeed, they exist at all.

George Bluestone, whose *Novels into Film* is a basic study of the relationship between fiction and film, suggests that "it is as fruitless to say that film A is better or worse than novel B as it is to pronounce Frank Lloyd Wright's Johnson's Wax Building better or worse than Tchaikowsky's *Swan Lake*."[1] George W. Linden agrees with Bluestone and blames this confusion of two art forms on the average viewer, who sees little difference between a novel and a film: "If he has not read the novel, he will consider himself to have read it after watching the film. If he has previously read the novel, he will either criticize the film for not being faithful to the book or praise it for being a fine rendering of the original."[2] In either case, Linden believes that the viewer's response would be invalid because it is based on an incorrect assumption that novels and films are the same.

Both Bluestone and Linden, among others, believe that a clearer distinction between prose fiction and film would be an important

[1]George Bluestone, *Novels Into Film*, 2nd ed. (Berkeley, Calif.: University of California Press, 1966), pp. 5–6. Excerpts from this book reprinted by permission of The Johns Hopkins Press.

[2]George W. Linden, *Reflections on the Screen* (Belmont, Calif.: Wadsworth Publishing Co., 1970), p. 34. Reprinted by permission of the publisher.

first step toward a deeper understanding of the connections between the art forms. However, two of our great contemporary filmmakers doubt that there are meaningful connections. Jean-Luc Godard (*Breathless*, 1959) expressed in an amazing fashion his concern over the difficulty of adapting a novel to the screen when an interviewer questioned him on the subject; Godard responded with a plan to visually reproduce the physical book on the screen, page by page.[3] Ingmar Bergman (*The Seventh Seal*, 1956) reacted in an even more outspoken fashion:

> Film has nothing to do with literature; the character and substance of the two art forms are usually in conflict. . . .
>
> We should avoid making films out of books. The irrational dimension of a literary work, the germ of its existence, is often untranslatable into visual terms— and it, in turn, destroys the special, irrational dimensions of the film. If, despite this, we wish to translate something literary into film terms, we must make an infinite number of complicated adjustments which often bear little or no fruit in proportion to the effort expended.[4]

Godard and Bergman, realizing the pitfalls of attempting film adaptations of works of literature, believe that it is better not to try than to botch things. We shall see that there is some truth in what they say, but both directors *have* made films based on literary sources. The plot of Bergman's *The Virgin Spring* (1959) was taken from "The Daughter of Tore in Vange," a thirteenth-century ballad read by the director as a university student.[5] Godard's *Masculin-Feminin* (1966) was based on two Maupassant stories, "The Signal" and "Paul's Mistress," and *Pierrot Le Fou* (1965)

[3]Walter S. Ross, "Splicing Together Jean-Luc Godard," *Esquire* (July 1969): 42.

[4]Ingmar Bergman, "Introduction," *Four Screenplays of Ingmar Bergman*, trans. Lars Malmstrom and David Kushner (New York: Simon and Schuster, 1960), pp. 17–18. © 1960 by Ingmar Bergman, reprinted by permission of Simon & Schuster.

[5]Brigitta Steene, *Ingmar Bergman* (New York: Twayne Publishers, Inc., 1968), p. 89.

made use of *Obsession*, a pulp detective novel by Lionel White.[6] In fact, it is hard to find a major living director who has not made at least one film from a literary work. Here are several examples that come to mind: Antonioni (*Blow-Up*, 1966), Bunuel (*Belle De Jour*, 1967), Fellini (*Satyricon*, 1969), Kurosawa (*The Throne of Blood* [*Macbeth*], 1957), Ray (*Pather Panchali*, 1955), Truffaut (*Jules and Jim*, 1961), Welles (*The Magnificent Ambersons*, 1942). While many films by our modern directors are based on original scripts, often written by themselves, it seems clear that a consideration of the relationship between the literary work and the film adaptation is still very relevant because of the number of films derived from literary works that are produced each year.

Estimating the percentage of total film production based on literary works has proven to be a popular and harmless game played by film historians. General estimates have been from 17 to nearly 50 percent.[7] Lester Asheim found that between 1935 and 1945, the major studios derived 17.2 percent of their films from novels alone.[8] Of the 305 films reviewed by the Production Code Office in 1955, 51.8 percent were derived from original source material.[9] In 1967 Harry M. Geduld estimated that around 40 percent of the Hollywood product has been based on literary works.[10]

When one considers the various reasons that directors and producers have for making film adaptations, it is fair to say that there will always be a significant portion of films based on literature, say at least 35 percent. The following review of Hollywood's use of literary adaptations will present these reasons in an historical context.

[6]Ian Cameron, ed., *The Films of Jean-Luc Godard* (New York: Frederick A. Praeger, Inc., Publishers, 1970), p. 187.

[7]Bluestone, p. 3.

[8]*"From Book to Film,"* Diss. University of Chicago 1949. Quoted in Bluestone, p. 3.

[9]Bluestone, p. 3.

[10]Harry M. Geduld, ed., *Film Makers on Film Making* (Bloomington, Ind.: Indiana University Press, 1969), p. 12.

I

Historians have been hesitant to be very specific about the earliest period of the theatrical film, due to the often contradictory facts that have been offered, but most agree that between 1895 and 1905 filmmaking evolved from very short plotless films to crude story productions. The earliest moviegoers were content to see simple static shots of moving objects. When Thomas Edison's Vitascope show opened at Koster and Bial's Music Hall in New York on April 23, 1896, viewers were treated to fifty-second films of sea waves, boxers, and scenes of Venice. Films such as these have their obvious limitations. By the turn of the century, the audience for a film of sea waves and the like had understandably diminished and producers turned to news events, travelogues, and variety acts in an attempt to pep up their presentations. During this period film length changed as well, from fifty-second "shorts" to full reels. (A reel runs about fourteen minutes.) Some have even suggested that several films may have run over an hour.[11] Few films, however, were longer than one reel in length.

There are two technical reasons that account for the limited use of literary sources in films around the turn of the century: first, most films were static camera, single-shot presentations; secondly, individual film length severely limited the literary works that could be adequately presented. Films based on literature were predominantly static documents of scenes from drama. As examples, Joseph Jefferson, the great American comic, played a few scenes from his stage hit "Rip Van Winkle" (1896), and the famous May Irwin–John C. Rice "Kiss" (1896) was actually a short excerpt from a popular play of the time, *The Widow Jones*.[12]

In the early 1900s Georges Méliès and Edwin S. Porter created new techniques that eventually brought part of the lost audience back into the theaters. While Méliès, a Frenchman, worked with a static camera, his films were usually narrative plots that told a

[11]Kenneth Macgowan, *Behind the Screen* (New York: Dell Publishing Co., 1967), pp. 84–89.

[12]Arthur Knight, *The Liveliest Art* (New York: The Macmillan Co., 1957), p. 14.

story: pantomimed tales such as "Cinderella" (1900) and "Red Riding Hood" (1901) gave impetus to the idea of story films. In this country, Porter's "Uncle Tom's Cabin" (1903) followed the directions and techniques exemplified by Méliès. Porter, however, is best known for his early experiments with editing techniques. While the shots were almost always static, Porter was able to cut from scene to scene, showing the development of actions happening parallel in time. The use of this editing technique is of prime importance to the history of cinema to this day and is of major importance with respect to the use of film adaptations of literature. Porter, however, saw little reason to use literary sources for his plots, since copyright laws for films did not exist and filmmakers freely plagiarized from one another.[13]

Still, the middle class in general and the more intelligent viewers in particular were in no great rush to flock back to the theaters to view rather simple narrative films. In 1907, a French company called Film d'Art attempted to draw this group into the general film audience by presenting films of staged plays. This venture was such a success that the company soon found itself turning to novels for source material. Most historians believe that this first extensive use of literary material can be attributed, in some degree, to snob appeal. Arthur Knight explains:

> People who would never have dreamed of going to the nickelodeons to see a cowboy picture, a tear-stained melodrama or a slapstick comedy, somehow felt that movies must be all right if they showed you the classics. For the first time the "right people" began to venture gingerly into the dark, grubby little theaters to see these new "artistic" films.[14]

At around this time, some American producers began to make films of the literary classics, partly due to the lead of the Film d'Art, partly as a response to the growing feeling that many films should be censored.[15] Thus, the filming of a literary classic was thought to

[13]Knight, pp. 15–18.

[14]Knight, p. 21.

[15]Lewis Jacobs, *The Rise of the American Film*, 2nd ed. (New York: Teachers College Press, Columbia University, 1968), p. 76. Excerpts from this book reprinted by permission of the author.

be both marketable and "respectable." However, the credit for presenting an American series of films based on the pattern of Film d'Art should go to Adolph Zukor and his Famous Players Company. In 1912 Zukor purchased the Film d'Art version of *Queen Elizabeth* starring Sarah Bernhardt, one of the leading actresses of the time. This four-reel film was first presented in July of that year in New York City and audiences paid an unheard of sum—$1.00—to see their first feature film.[16] The experiment was such a success that Zukor started the Famous Players Company with E. S. Porter as director. Other feature-length film organizations were quickly started on the same premise; in 1913 audiences were very receptive to the many filmed plays screened throughout the nation.[17]

While 1906–16 is thought of as the period in which the story film gained the ascendance enjoyed today, the production of story films longer than one reel was severely restricted because of a film trust composed of the major producers and distributors known as the Motion Picture Patents Company. This film trust attempted to control the industry from the making of a film to its projection in the theater and had decided that audiences would not sit through a film of more than one reel in duration. Because of the restrictions of the film trust, there were relatively few attempts to make films based on full-length literary works. However, by 1912 the country began to consider the problems of trusts and in 1913 the Patents Company was brought into court as an alleged violator of the Sherman anti-trust law.[18] Thus, from 1912 on, independent filmmakers outside of the control of Patents Company began to make longer films with the knowledge that the distributors of their films would not be harrassed by Patents Company "goon squads," a fact of life prior to that time. This opened the door to film adaptations of a more appropriate length; films could be made of complete novels, plays, and narrative poems rather than scenes from them. Such earlier absurdities as *Hamlet* in ten minutes were seldom repeated.[19]

[16]Knight, pp. 22–23. Also, see Macgowan, pp. 157–58.
[17]Jacobs, p. 91.
[18]Jacobs, p. 84.
[19]Knight, p. 22.

D. W. Griffith's version of Tennyson's "Enoch Arden" (1911)
is considered to be the first two-reel American film to be screened
at a single showing, but the early emphasis on feature productions
came from abroad, where film trusts had never dictated film length,
and these films were often adaptations of novels. The eight-reel
Italian *The Last Days of Pompeii* (1911) and two 1913 French
features, *Germinal* (eight reels), and *Les Miserables* (twelve reels),
were early indications of the trend.[20] These continental novel-films
were very popular in America, and American filmmakers went on
to spend large sums for various novel rights. Griffith's *The Birth
of a Nation* (1915), taken from Thomas Dixon's *The Clansman*,
garnered the highest royalty of that era. Dixon was paid $260,000
plus 25 percent interest in the film's returns.[21]

D. W. Griffith's place in the history of the film is assured, and
one of his many contributions to the medium is the example he
set for future filmmakers who wished to adapt a work of literature
to film. Griffith became a filmmaker after a financially unsuccessful
attempt at writing and acting. At seventeen he was a reporter for
the Louisville *Courier*, and he soon took to the road as a traveling
actor. He wrote plays, short stories, and poems; his poems and
stories were published in such magazines as *Colliers*, *Good House-
keeping*, and *Cosmopolitan* and one play, *A Fool and a Girl*, was
presented in Washington and Baltimore for a two-week period
during 1907 but gained a cool reception.[22] As for his reading, he
was particularly interested in the Victorians; Tennyson, Browning,
and Dickens were favorites. Griffith began directing films in 1908.
Obviously, his literary interests and abilities were richly rewarded
in a medium just learning to use the art of narrative. Lewis Jacobs
theorizes that Griffith made great use of literary works not for
their snob appeal nor for their obvious attraction as "pre-sold"
vehicles, but for reasons that suggest the man's faith in the artistic
possibilities of the then-infant medium:

> Griffith realized that pictures could become significant
> only if their content was significant. He therefore led a
> raid on the classics for his material. Before his first year

[20]Macgowan, pp. 156–57.
[21]Jacobs, p. 218.
[22]Jacobs, p. 97.

as a movie director was ended, he had not only adapted works by Jack London and Tennyson but had boldly brought to the screen Shakespeare, Hood, Tolstoy, Poe, O. Henry, Reade, Maupassant, Stevenson, Browning. Among the hundred or so pictures of this first year were "The Taming of the Shrew," "The Song of the Shirt," "Resurrection," "Edgar Allan Poe," "The Cricket on the Hearth," "The Necklace," "Suicide Club," and "The Lover's Tale."[23]

Griffith continued to "raid" literary sources throughout his career. Since he was considered the master director of his time, one can easily understand why the vast majority of filmgoers thought that the relationship between literature and film was quite close.

By the end of World War I, film had become *the* mass public entertainment. So many films were being turned out to meet the demand that literary sources were ransacked rather than raided, as producers attempted to feed the hungry maw of an industry in search of a plot. Other than in comedy, gone were the days of plotting when someone on the studio lot could suggest a premise and have a group of actors improvise upon the idea in front of a camera (although there are indications that such techniques are presently being resurrected, sometimes advantageously). Writing for the screen was a serious, well-paying profession, and articles on the art of writing for film were written for such magazines as *Photoplay* and *Motion Picture Classic*.[24]

As filmmaking geared itself for industrial output, film adaptations of literary works suffered in new ways. Kevin Brownlow has described the custom in *The Parade's Gone By....* When the work was purchased, it immediately became a property. The property was then compressed into a brief synopsis for a reading by the producer who, more often than not, had never read the work. If the producer liked the synopsis, the property was given to a writer who worked it into a scenario. The emphasis in the scenario was on the visual elements of the work. The property then went through the hands of various supervisors, directors, actors, heads, agents, rewrite men, and the like until a finished product was

[23]Jacobs, p. 104.
[24]Jacobs, p. 219.

readied for shooting. There were "many versions, many concep-
tions—all of them a compromise between literary convention and
cinematic compression, all of them involving further creative
blood-lettings."[25] On occasion, even the author of the literary work
gave his assistance to the project.[26]

In 1921, Paramount devised a method that, in a sense, attempted
to eliminate the middleman, the professional screen writer. The
plan was summed up in the following advertisement:

> The greatest living authors are now working with Para-
> mount. Sir James Barrie you know; and Joseph Conrad,
> Arnold Bennett, Robert Hitchens, E. Phillips Oppen-
> heim, Sir Gilbert Parker, Elinor Glyn, Edward Knob-
> lock, W. Somerset Maugham, Avery Hopwood, Henry
> Arthur Jones, Cosmo Hamilton, Edward Sheldon, Sam-
> uel Merwin, Harry J. O'Higgens—all of these famous
> authors are actually in the studios writing new plays
> for Paramount Pictures, advising with directors, using
> the motion picture camera as they formerly used a
> pen.[27]

This group was called Eminent Authors Inc. but, as Brownlow
explains, "some of the scenarios written by the Eminent Authors
have remained in Hollywood legend as Awful Examples."[28] Thus,
we can see that filmscripts by committee have severe limitations
when it comes to adapting literature for the screen and that there
is no guarantee that writers of great literature are able to produce
acceptable filmscripts.

With the coming of sound in the late twenties, writing for the
screen became even more difficult. In his biography of Irving

[25]Kevin Brownlow, *The Parade's Gone By . . .* (New York, Bal-
lantine Books, Inc., 1969), p. 311.
[26]Lillian Ross' *Picture* is a fine account of the system and is considered a classic work of cinema reportage. The book deals with
The Red Badge of Courage as it progressed from a Crane novel
to a John Huston film. Many examples of conflicts between
writers, producers, and directors are presented. The book is also
an interesting example of the factual report as novel, a form that
has presently been made famous by Capote's *In Cold Blood* and
Mailer's *The Armies of the Night*.
[27]Jacobs, p. 326.
[28]Brownlow, p. 315.

Thalberg, the production manager of MGM until his death in 1936, Bob Thomas discusses the power of the script writer in the early talkies:

> With the coming of sound, Thalberg's relationships with writers intensified. The exigencies of dialogue called for more careful preparation of scripts; no longer could areas of action remain vague, to be interpreted by the director as he saw fit. Now the writer was ascendant, and the position of the director at M-G-M declined.[29]

While dramatic works benefited most from talkies, for obvious reasons, the number of novels made into films did not diminish. The extra dimension of spoken dialogue added to the other novelistic elements capable of being reproduced in the film. The script writer's task as adapter became more difficult and, consequently, he became more important with respect to the value of the finished product. One side effect of this new importance was that the literature from which the films were adapted was treated with a bit more respect, and the films tended to be more successful as adaptations. Naturally, some of this success must be attributed to the inclusion of sound, but the new attitudes about the value of the screenplay could not help but influence attitudes toward the literary work.

The power of the Hollywood studio system increased through the thirties, and, by the forties, the total preëminence of the studio product became a fact of life. The financial strength of the industry, with its increased attendance, enabled such powers as MGM and Paramount to attract many of the literary greats. Fitzgerald, Hemingway, and Faulkner wrote for films at one time or another. With the European disaster of the thirties and forties, writers such as Isherwood, Huxley, and Brecht found themselves in Los Angeles.

In *Hollywood in the Forties*, Charles Higham and Joel Greenberg describe the climate of the time that produced some respectable film adaptations. The studios, feeling financially secure, grew

---

[29]Bob Thomas, *Thalberg: Life and Legend* (New York: Bantam Books, 1970), p. 165.

more willing to invest money in "prestige" films. The major studios' producers, directors, actors and actresses, set designers, and writers were put to work turning out "serious" films based on literary "classics": "The surprising thing throughout the decade is that the classics should have been exploited with so great a measure of artistic success."[30]

During the thirties and forties, the script writer was often thought of as being more important than the director. Some writers, Preston Sturges (*Sullivan's Travels*, 1942), for example, later became directors on the strength of their script writing. At present, however, we are in the era of the director. Most major directors collaborate with their writers on the scripts; some, particularly the foreign directors, simply write the scripts themselves. Others, to quote the French filmmaker and critic, Alexander Astruc, write with a "*camera-stylo*" (camera-pen):

> This of course implies that the scriptwriter directs his own scripts; or rather, that the scriptwriter ceases to exist, for in this kind of film-making the distinction between author and director loses all meaning. Direction is no longer a means of illustrating or presenting a scene, but a true act of writing. The filmmaker/author writes with his camera as a writer writes with his pen.[31]

This idea partly accounts for the views expressed by Godard and Bergman noted earlier. However, the concept of the *camera-stylo* is an ideal rather than a norm, and it remains to be seen whether literary adaptations, by their very nature, prevent the filmmaker from recognizing his full artistic capabilities in the film medium.

While one might think that such current facts of life as the rise of the international cinema, the young independent filmmakers in America, and the waning of the Hollywood studios would naturally lead to more personal films, that is, more films with original scripts, this is not necessarily the case. What we

[30]Charles Higham and Joel Greenberg, *Hollywood in the Forties* (London: The Tantivy Press, 1968), p. 105.

[31]Alexandre Astruc, "The Birth of a New Avant-Garde: La Camera-Stylo," *The New Wave*, ed. Peter Graham (Garden City, N. Y.: Doubleday and Co., Inc., 1968), p. 22. This essay was written for *Ecran Français* and appeared in 1948.

know at this point is that the main reasons for using literature as film sources have been with us since nearly the beginnings of film and will probably continue to be evident in the future. The artistic value and publicized title of the original literary works, particularly novels, are "pre-sold." Also, there are presently a number of examples of a "spinoff" trend, the novel written after the fact of the film; Erich Segal's bestseller, *Love Story* (1970), grew out of his film scenario and its commercial success is in turn helping to sell the film. As Otto Preminger (*Exodus*, 1960) has said with respect to *Love Story*, "There are two advertising media. One is the bestseller. The other is TV."[32] Whether the film is adapted from the novel or, in some cases, the novel is adapted from the scenario of the film, Preminger's point is well taken. According to Joseph Gelmis, some movie companies have helped to make bestsellers out of novels to which they own film rights. Gelmis notes that film company employees were given money to purchase numerous copies of *Love Story*, *Rosemary's Baby*, and *The Godfather* in markets that influence the bestseller lists published by several newspapers.[33]

Aside from the "pre-sold" literary classic and the bestseller as an advertisement for the film, history offers the following explanations for film adaptations of literary works: films based on literature have a certain snob appeal and often are used to bolster the sometimes sagging cultural posture of the industry as a purveyor of art; many who have not read the literary work will want to see the film to catch up culturally; literature offers ready-made plots and themes for producers and directors hard put to come up with an original idea; adaptations offer highly creative challenges to filmmakers willing to take the risk of failure. In most cases, the reasons are undoubtedly a combination of these as well as others of a more idiosyncratic nature.[34]

[32]"Three Gatherings," *The New Yorker* (January 30, 1971): 22.
[33]Joseph Gelmis, "Exhibitionists and the Games They Play," *New York* (August 31, 1970): 58.
[34]A particular piece of literature might be considered a "perfect" vehicle for a particular star (Elizabeth Taylor as Cleopatra). Or, a particular director or producer might have certain literary favorites that he would enjoy turning into films. (Godard has said that he would like to make a film based on a novel by Thomas Hardy. [!])

No matter what reason a filmmaker has for adapting a literary work to the film medium, his decision to do so should lead him to consider the relationship between literature and film. The next section will treat some significant aesthetic theories dealing with this relationship and will outline a theory of adaptation, particularly with respect to prose fiction.

II

Art forms always attract critical minds who enjoy analyzing, commenting upon, and theorizing about the works of the artists. In some cases the artists themselves take on the role of theorists. In literature, John Dryden and T. S. Eliot may serve as examples; in film, Sergei Eisenstein and the New Wave director-critics (Godard, Truffaut, Chabrol) could be seen in the same light. More often than not, major directors, like major writers, do not take on the role of the critic for any extended time; such intellectually stimulating work is usually done by men who consider themselves to be practicing theorists rather than professional filmmakers. However, as in so many cases when it comes to matters of general film theory, one of the first major evaluations concerning the relationship between prose fiction and film was advanced by Eisenstein in an essay written in 1944, "Dickens, Griffith, and the Film Today." This important essay refutes one of three major assumptions concerning the relationship between literature and film.

The film audience has traditionally assumed that drama is closer to the art of film than prose fiction or poetry. Hollywood tended to hold this assumption at least twice during its brief history: many of the earliest story films were excerpts of plays, and with the advent of sound in the late twenties and early thirties, dramatists, stage directors, and stage actors and actresses flooded Hollywood and were given high-paying jobs. As the silent film developed as an art, and as the sound film has similarly evolved, there have been definite moves away from the drama form as a cinema aesthetic. The reasons for this are implicit in Eisenstein's essay, and it is far from coincidental that he finds his proof in the work of D. W. Griffith.

The very heart of the art of the film is its ability to change visual viewpoints of static or moving objects in time and space. This is done through film editing or cutting aided by the moving camera, and Griffith was the first to use all of the basic editing and moving camera techniques with a high degree of artistic control. Eisenstein theorizes that Griffith developed his techniques through his reading of narrative prose, particularly Dickens' novels. The use of close-ups, parallel editing sequences, intercuts, fades, dissolves, camera angles, pans, and tracks can be found in a film such as *Intolerance* (1916), and these techniques are all to be found in novels rather than plays.[35] A. B. Walkley reported the following in the *Times* of London, April 26, 1922:

> He [Griffith] is a pioneer, by his own admission, rather than an inventor. That is to say, he has opened up new paths in Film Land, under the guidance of ideas supplied to him from outside. His best ideas, it appears, have come to him from Dickens, who has always been his favorite author. . . . Dickens inspired Mr. Griffith with an idea, and his employers (mere "business" men) were horrified at it; but, says Mr. Griffith, "I went home, re-read one of Dicken's novels, and came back next day to tell them they could either make use of my idea or dismiss me."[36]

Such an insight into Griffith's use of literary sources accounts for his various literary adaptations as well. While he surely attempted to do justice to the literature, it is clear that particular works were chosen because of the technical problems they presented. For example, Griffith's company, Biograph, was very hesitant in allowing him to make a film based on Browning's poem, "Pippa Passes." The director was most insistent. Given the innovations in lighting that resulted through the aid of his cameraman,

[35]For a description of these techniques, see the introductory material before the shot analysis.

[36]Sergei Eisenstein, "Dickens, Griffith, and the Film Today," *Film Form* (New York: Harcourt, Brace and Co., Inc., 1949), p. 205.

Billy Bitzer, it is easy to understand the attraction of a poem in four parts that would demand lighting for scenes taking place during the morning, at noon, through the evening, and at night.[37] Using literary sources for such experiments, Griffith eventually produced all of the major film techniques. In particular, works of narrative prose fiction helped him to make film a narrative art.

Based on Griffith's experiences with film adaptation of prose, we may conclude the following about film narration. Through editing and the moving camera, a film may jump forward and backward in time, move from one scene to another in space, look at a scene from a distance, shift to a closeup of a particular detail in the scene, and look at it from a number of different angles. Obviously, the drama cannot do all of these things since the viewer is seated at a fixed point in the auditorium and can view the event on the stage from only one angle. Thus, with respect to similar narrative techniques, prose fiction should be easier to adapt to the screen than drama.

The second incorrect assumption held by many moviegoers is that film communicates the same kinds of information as prose fiction and does so in the same way. In *Novels into Film*, George Bluestone addresses himself to this misconception by outlining the different ways fiction and film produce meaning. Bluestone believes that the most obvious difference between film and literature is that film presents a photographic reproduction of physical reality, whereas language alludes to this reality through the use of verbal symbols. Prose fiction is made up of words that are imaginatively perceived by the reader through a thought process, but film demands no cognition since the information is directly perceived.[38] Consider this as an example:

> If I say, "The top spins on the table," my mind assembles first the top, then the spinning, then the table. . . . But on the screen, I simply perceive a shot of a top spinning on a table. . . .[39]

This difference is most apparent, and quite crucial, when we

[37]Jacobs, pp. 107–108.
[38]Bluestone, pp. 20–24.
[39]Bluestone, p. 59.

consider one of the basic tools of literary communication, the metaphor. Language is highly connotative, while film is not; hence, a literary work that places an emphasis upon metaphor would seem inappropriate as a source of film adaptation. Virginia Woolf has commented upon this:

> Even the simplest image: "my love's like a red, red rose, that's newly sprung in June," presents us with impressions of moisture and warmth and the flow of crimson and the softness of petals inextricably mixed and strung upon the life of a rhythm which is itself the voice of the passion and the hesitation of the love. All this, which is accessible to words alone, the cinema must avoid.[40]

Interestingly, some writers are disturbed about the built-in flux of meaning in language, and have attempted to present the "truth" of reality by eliminating connotation. Given the nature of language, such attempts are doomed to failure, and one suspects that these writers are well aware of this and include such an understanding in their literary strategies. Alain Robbe-Grillet has written works calculated to attack this limitation of language and it is not surprising that his novels have been called "cinematic," that his short story collection is titled *Snapshots*, and that he is presently making feature-length films.

However, most of us would be inclined to think that Virginia Woolf's comment upon film limitation is more telling than Robbe-Grillet's correct assumption about the nature of language. We are willing to live with connotative language because words render a rich imaginative experience. On the other hand, we might wish that the rendering of experience through direct visualizations could be more imaginatively stimulating than it is. This, I suspect, is one of the reasons so many viewers are dissatisfied with films made from great literary works.

This is not to say that filmmakers have not tried to reproduce metaphor in film. Bluestone notes that montage offers the director a unique cinematic tool that can be used for an effect analogous

---

[40]Virginia Woolf, "The Movies and Reality," *New Republic*, 4 (August 4, 1926): 309. Quoted in Bluestone, p. 21.

to the literary metaphor.[41] Through editing, film is able to jump from one action to another and from one object to another, making contrasting comments with somewhat the same effect as figurative language. Still, the effect is analogous but not equal, for words produce richer webs of connotative information than montage images.

Other important distinctions made by Bluestone create this rule: fiction is better able to represent the interior realities of man, while film is more adept at presenting his exterior world. For example:

> The rendition of mental states—memory, dream, imagination—cannot be as adequately represented by film as by language. If the film has difficulty presenting streams of consciousness, it has even more difficulty presenting states of mind precisely by the absence in them of the visible world.[42]

We know of one instance where this view seems contradictory to that rule, the presentation of time. Time cannot literally be seen, but it can be perceived through dislocations of space. Hence, while modern novelists and story writers grow more and more interested in detailing man's interior world, they grow more and more frustrated in their attempts to place man in the flux of time. Here is where film has an edge over prose fiction. Through cinematic editing, double exposure, and the like, we are able to experience past, present, and future simultaneously in space, thus creating the illusion of the time flux. Language, being sequential, is unable to do this.[43]

Given all of the significant differences between novel and film, Bluestone understandably concludes that we have no right to expect the film to be like the novel because "the filmed novel, in spite of certain resemblances, will inevitably become a different artistic entity from the novel on which it is based."[44]

At this point, I should add that this discussion has been proceeding with the understanding that we have been considering the

[41]Bluestone, pp. 24–27.
[42]Bluestone, p. 47.
[43]Bluestone, pp. 48–61.
[44]Bluestone, p. 64.

difficulties inherent in adapting successful literary works of art to film. Many fine films have been based on poor novels: Ford's *The Informer* (1935), Visconti's *Ossessione* (*The Postman Always Rings Twice*, 1942), Nichols' *The Graduate* (1967). No one has ever complained that these films did not do justice to their respective books. In other words, those who invalidly complain that the film was not like the book characteristically feel the necessity to do so when a film has been made from an artfully successful literary product.

This fact of cinematic life leads to our consideration of the third, and last, incorrect assumption about literature and film: great literary works should never be adapted to film because such adaptations are doomed to failure. Obviously, it would be impossible for one person to hold both the second assumption as well as this third. Some err by assuming too many relationships between fiction and film, others, by assuming too few. John Dryden's comments on the art of literary translation found in his "Preface to Ovid's Epistles" (1680) can be used to suggest these positions on translating literature to film. Dryden reduces literary translation to three types:

> First, that of metaphrase, or turning an author word by word and line by line, from one language to another. . . . The second way is that of paraphrase or translation with latitude, where the author is kept in view by the translator, so as never to be lost, but his words are not so strictly followed as his sense, and that too is admitted to be amplified, but not altered. . . . The third way is that of imitation, where the translator . . . assumes the liberty not only to vary from the words and senses, but to forsake them both as he sees occasion; and taking only some general hints from the original, to run division on the groundwork as he pleases.[45]

Dryden dislikes metaphrase, for no language can adequately reproduce another, word for word, and he also dislikes imitation, for this allows the translator to write as a second author, to use the original "as a pattern, and to write, as he supposes that [original]

[45]John Dryden, *Of Dramatic Poesy and Other Critical Essays*, ed. George Watson (London: J. M. Dent and Sons, Ltd., 1962), I, p. 268.

author would have done, had he lived in our age, and in our country."[46] Dryden finds that the paraphrase exists as a sensible middle ground between these two extremes. The translator who paraphrases must be in control of the language of the original work as well as his own native tongue, must find a means of expressing the original as closely as possible without ruining the beauty of his own language, and must take great care that the sense of the original is retained—not part of the sense but *all* of it.

While we know that film adaptations are not literary translations, let us consider how Dryden's theory may apply to literature and film. Metaphrase is out of the question for the many reasons given by Bluestone; there is simply no way to change words to images as a metaphrase would demand. Imitation is another matter. Many films have been made that could be called imitations. In such films the literary works become "properties," and there is little or no attempt made to render a cinematic equivalent of the original. Such films might use part of the plot, some of the characters, and a theme or two from the original, but there are so many eliminations, changes, and additions that the sense of the original literary work is lost. On occasion, only the title of the original work is retained. Such films may or may not be successful works of cinematic art, but their worth will have nothing to do with their creative adaptation of the literary work. Many film "imitations" exist, and most are failures because the pragmatic reasons for the initial purchase of the "property" often are indicative of the tastes and values that govern the making of the finished film. Naturally, such films make it just that much harder for creative adaptations to be taken seriously.

It follows, then, that the artful film adaptation would be similar to Dryden's idea of a literary paraphrase. Unfortunately this is not quite the case, and it is for this reason that some assume that a valid film adaptation of a literary work is an impossibility. The film adapter could have a control of the art of language and the art of film; but, for reasons previously noted, while he could express some of the language cinematically, he could not express all of it. Further, while he could take great care to communicate

[46]Dryden, p. 270.

a sense of the original, he could not possibly express *all* the sense of the original. It is impossible for a two- or even three-hour film to duplicate a novel taking five to ten hours to read. Erich von Stroheim's *Greed* (1923) is the classic example of the results obtained from meeting this latter problem head-on. *Greed* is an adaptation of Frank Norris' naturalistic novel, *McTeague*. Stroheim attempted to produce a complete film version of the novel as well as some material of his own. The novel is over 300 pages long and the faithful translation produced seven and a half hours of finished edited film. Stroheim's additions brought the finished film up to forty-two reels (ten hours). MGM raged and had the director edit the film down to a more reasonable length for screening. Stroheim reduced the film to five hours; his friend, director Rex Ingram, lopped off an hour of that; and MGM, still not satisfied, gave it to a third party who had few ideas about Norris' novel and fewer about Stroheim's conception of it. The released version was two and one half hours in length.[47] The sixteen-mm rental print runs one hour and fifty-four minutes. It is to Stroheim's eternal credit that the film makes any sense at all! Clearly, the sense of the original has not been totally retained. Hence, even if we were to assume that the experience and ideas in a novel were not ever-lastingly confined by the inextricable web of the language, the conventions of film length are such that paraphrase is impossible.

But what of the short story? (For purposes of this discussion, the novella will be considered as a short novel or a long short story.) Theoretically, the limited material of the short story should enable the director to cover the various senses of a particular story in the length of a feature film. However, this is not the case, for the short story often gains its compression of material partly through a poetic use of language, and, as we know, film is limited in its ability to treat connotative language. Further, while the short story characteristically treats fewer sequences of actions, filmmakers tend to expand plot to the point that the feature film adapted from a short story will contain more original material than adapted material. Thus, the finished film is often "from" or "based on" or

[47]Joel W. Finler, *Stroheim* (Berkeley, Calif.: University of California Press, 1968), pp. 33–34.

"inspired by" the original rather than adapted. Finally, short story–films of less than feature length run afoul of the very same problems as novel-films.

Thus, using Dryden's description of types of translation, clearly one cannot translate a work of literature to film. However, those who assume that the literary work cannot be adapted into a film assume that the characteristic method of adaptation is translation. This is not the case. As George Linden suggests, the adaptation is a *transformation* rather than a translation.[48]

The key to transformation is analogy. Adaptation by analogy, incidentally, is nothing new, for this is the characteristic way artists have always adapted a work of art to another medium. Art forms are unique in the way that they communicate content; indeed, some hold that the content in one art form is untranslatable to another because the art form actually shapes the content. However, as Bela Balazs, the great Hungarian film critic, has pointed out, adaptations from one art form to another have been made successfully for centuries. The method is the same in all cases, and Balazs outlines it for film adaptations:

> To accept the thesis that the content or material determines the form and with it the art form, and nevertheless to admit the possibility of putting the same material into a different form, is thinkable only if the terms are used loosely, that is if the terms "content" and "form" do not exactly cover what we are accustomed to call material, action, plot, story, subject, etc. on the one hand and "art form" on the other. There can be no doubt that it is possible to take the subject, the story, the plot of a novel, turn it into a ... film and yet produce perfect works of art in each case—the form being in each case adequate to the content.... It is possible because, while the subject, or story, of both works is identical, their *content* is nevertheless different. It is this different *content* that is adequately expressed in the changing form resulting from the adaptation.[49]

[48]Linden, p. 35.

[49]Bela Balazs, *Theory of the Film*, trans. Edith Bone (London: Dennis Dobson, Ltd., 1952), pp. 259–60. Excerpts from this book reprinted by permission of the publisher.

The successful film adaptation of a novel must walk a thin line between expressing the values of the novel and expressing values that, while artfully done, have nothing to do with the novel. In terms of Dryden's idea of the translation, the film adaptation can be neither a paraphrase nor an imitation, but something in between. The film should not be evaluated on the basis of its faithfulness to all elements of the novel; neither should it be seen as an entity having nothing whatever to do with the original. Through analogy, film can suggest the values of a particular novel; however, because of the many limitations previously mentioned, film cannot do so totally. Hence, it must attempt to capture the spirit of the work. Linden has commented on this point:

> A director can change the plot of a novel, he can elim-inate certain characters and scenes, and he can include scenes not included in the novel without violating it. But he cannot seriously violate the theme of the novel, and the one thing he must be able to translate into his new medium is its tone. . . . Of course, if the director succeeds in his effort, he will have produced not a copy of the novel, but a new object: an art film that aims at close targets in a different way.[50]

Linden suggests that Martin C. Battestin's essay "Osborne's *Tom Jones*: Adapting a Classic" is a fine example of an application of the proper criteria for film adaptation. This essay is well-suited to our purposes, particularly since Battestin is a representative of that profession that too often assumes that film adaptations of literary classics are doomed to failure. He is a professor of English and a Henry Fielding scholar. Further, his credentials are impeccable: he has written a book on Fielding's art and has edited a number of the novels. Too often in the past, such a scholar would be quite hesitant to praise a film version of a work by a writer in his chosen literary field. Naturally, no film would be able to capture the total meaning of the literary work, and scholars have been heard to say ". . . must be turning over in his grave!" or, "If only . . . were alive today to see this!" Thus, the case for the creation of an artful film adaptation through analogy is quite strong when a Fielding scholar

[50]Linden, p. 49.

is able to praise the film version of *Tom Jones* (1963) as "...a splendid illustration of what can be done in the intelligent adaptation of fiction to the screen."[51] Battestin, however, has not closed his eyes to the limitations of the film: he is aware that *Tom Jones* does not reproduce every character and scene to be found in the original; he even concludes that the film hardly captures the moral vision of the novel. However, in Battestin's eyes, the film succeeds in spite of this: "If Osborne [the scriptwriter] and Richardson [the director] missed a major intention behind Fielding's novel, they fully grasped and brilliantly recreated its essential spirit and manner."[52] This cinematic success is achieved through analogy:

> Analogy is the key. To judge whether or not a film is a successful adaptation of a novel is to evaluate the skill of its makers in striking analogous attitudes and in finding analogous rhetorical techniques.[53]

III

Having considered the inherent difficulties of adapting a literary work to film and having constructed a general theory of how such adaptations may be done, one pragmatic question remains: how may one determine the success or failure of a particular film adaptation? First of all, one should have a clear knowledge of what the literary work is doing and how these ends are achieved. In the case of this book, the criticism found immediately after the short story should help to develop an interpretation. Secondly, one should have an equally lucid view of the values of the film and its methods of achievement. Again, in terms of this book, the criticism on the film placed after the shot analysis should be of aid. (Since the shot analysis is an interpretive transcript of the finished film rather than a pre-film shooting script or pre-film scenario, its im-

[51]Martin C. Battestin, "Osborne's *Tom Jones:* Adapting a Classic," *Man and the Movies,* ed. W. R. Robinson (Baton Rouge: Louisiana State University Press, 1967), p. 45. Reprinted by permission of the publisher.

[52]Battestin, p. 36.

[53]Battestin, p. 37.

portance will become clear as one works on the relationships between story and film.)

After developing an interpretation of both the story and the film, the next step should be a consideration of the worth of the film as an adaptation. At this point, the basic criterion for adaptation should be kept in mind: a successful adaptation will reproduce as much of the spirit and as many of the themes of the original as possible given the limitations of the film medium. The film may eliminate part of the plot or a number of the characters of the original work; it may even add plot sequences and characters as it sees fit. Such decisions are perfectly acceptable as long as a serious distortion of the original does not result. Finally, one should remember that the successful adaptation gains many of these ends through analogous techniques. While both Linden and Battestin have made this point, it is well to remember that some elements of prose fiction can readily be adapted to film without the need for transformation of the material through analogy. On the other hand, other prose fiction elements cannot be transformed into cinematic devices so readily. To suggest how all of this works, brief comments on the relationship between specific devices found in prose fiction and film will follow. Since several fiction/film devices have already been discussed at some length, some of the comments will be made in the form of summary statements.

PLOT

Since plot in fiction is an artful selection of meaningful representative actions, it is relatively easy to duplicate in a film. Plot usually consists of a beginning, that is, a stasis point, a kind of fixed order; a middle, a conflict of two forces that threaten to break up the ordered norm; and an end, the resolution of this conflict.

Naturally, there are ordinarily many more representative actions in the novel than in the short story. When a film is adapted from a novel, the representative actions must, of necessity, be limited. While the short story usually contains fewer actions, the film adaptation usually is presented in a shorter period of actual screen time, thus creating virtually the same problem as the treatment of plot in the novel; the other alternative would be to have the film expand upon the plot itself. There are very few cases where the film adaptation of a story chooses to present only the actions portrayed in the story in a full-length (ninety-minute) work, most likely because the short story tends toward poetic compression and the film is unable to expand these elements to make up for the limitation of action. Thus, a film adaptation of a literary plot may eliminate some actions and add others, the rule being that the adaptation should be as artfully representative and selective in terms of the raw material of the literary work as that work was representative and selective of the raw materials of reality. Finally, it must be remembered that the basic difference between prose narrative and film narrative is that what the words do in prose the film usually does in images.

CHARACTER

There are two basic characters in film as well as in prose —the protagonist, that person who represents the positive values in the story, and the antagonist, that person in conflict with him. In order for the audience or the reader to identify with the protagonist and feel threatened by the antagonist, the characters must be well-rounded—enough information must be given about them so that they become believable to us. Other flatter characters may surround these two in such a way that a fully realized world is presented. Sometimes such characters are foils, characters who are compared with or contrasted to the protagonist or antagonist in ways that help to define their characters. On other occasions, some of the flatter characters serve to represent particular value systems or cultural points of view that help to make the main conflict understandable. As in our consideration of plot, it is easy to see that the novel can develop a more complex network of various characters than the short story or film. Further, there will also be a tendency toward static characterization in the short story and film for much the same reasons. However, the short story is able to produce rounded, dynamic characterizations through a careful selection of plot incidents and character details as well as through language compression, a tactic that is of limited use to the film-maker. This problem may be partly resolved through analogy:

> The gestures of visual man are not intended to convey concepts which can be expressed in words, but such inner experiences, such nonrational emotions which would still remain unexpressed when everything that can be told has been told.[54]

While the director may be unable to express the wealth of detail needed for a rounded character found in the successful prose narrative, he can make use of the visual dramatization produced by the actors and actresses themselves, something prose fiction cannot do.

Ultimately, whether we are reading about characters or watching them on the screen, their actions and character changes must be plausible (believable), consistent (compatible with their personalities), and motivated (they should act for a valid reason). Too often in the past, film characterizations have not been as strong as those found in prose fiction. This, in part at least, explains the hold the star system has had over films, particularly in this country. Typically, the director is able to use actors and actresses with identifiable screen characters developed over the years. A Bogart, a Brando, a Monroe, or a Loren is able to play a type developed during the course of many films, and the lazy director relies upon typecasting to carry the weight of the characterization. While the star system will always be with us to some extent, the film today is more willing to rely upon the artistry needed to produce a well-rounded character in a particular film. It must be remembered that film is in its infancy relative to the literary arts. In a sense, the history of film in terms of characterization can be seen as similar to early folk literature where types and stock characterizations are to be found in abundance. However, gone are the days of "good guys" and "bad guys" as staples of film characterization. Finally, one other limitation of film characterization should be mentioned.

[54]Balazs, p. 40.

If an author were interested in developing the interior world of a character, the film would have some difficulty in portraying it. Hence, this limitation should be considered when evaluating the success of character adaptation.

SETTING

The physical locale against which the plot is developed and the characters operate is called setting. Its function is three-fold in that it partly controls the characters, suggests the theme (idea expressed by the work), and produces an atmosphere. Since setting is governed by plot, at least in part, it is an effective way to control our responses to the action. As plot is an artful selection of incidents, setting is an artful selection of the physical environment in which the plot takes place. However, while the writer is able to select elements within a particular scene to reinforce character, theme, and atmosphere and still produce a feeling of verisimilitude, the film customarily reproduces the realistic physicality of the scene, but much of the artful selection made by the writer is sometimes left to the audience. The problem here is found in a conflict of conventions. Realistic prose works do not operate like realistic films in this respect. On the other hand, expressionistic settings in fiction, that is, settings expressive of a character's inner state or attitude, can be duplicated in film. Thus, the director's most difficult task is to attempt to reproduce a selective but realistic locale without producing an expressionistic setting.

POINT OF VIEW

The plot of a prose work is mainly narrated from the point of view of an unidentified speaker outside the story or from the point of view of a character within the story. The outside narrator is either omniscient, one who has a total knowledge of the facts and can narrate this information either from the outside or inside of the particular characters to be found in any time and any place, or limited, one who is only privy to the facts known by one character in the story. In either case, the plot is narrated in the third person. If the story is told from the point of view of a character within the story itself, the reader is not only limited to the knowledge that the particular character is privy to, but the narrative is recounted in the actual words of that character. Such a point of view is called first-person narration.

On occasion, writers as diverse as Isherwood, Mann, and Robbe-Grillet have employed a "camera" point of view in which the material is presented in a totally objective manner exactly as a camera would record a situation. Also, while short stories tend to be presented from one point of view throughout, some novels, such as Joyce's *Ulysses*, mix first-person and third-person points of view. Since the writer is free to select a particular point of view or even a particular combination of points of view for a given story, such a selection becomes an important element in the art of the work. Many works have been weakened by a poor selection of point of view.

Film does not have the luxury of succeeding with as many points of view. It follows, then, that the quality of some literary works is not accessible to film. With care, an acceptable third-person-limited film can be made, but film customarily is narrated from a third-person-omniscient point of view. In such cases, the camera shifts back and forth from the role of detached observer (objective) to the point of view of one of the participants (subjective). Total "camera" films or totally subjective films are seldom successful, particularly as features, due to the monotony of the approaches. Although a number of films have been adapted from novels and short stories narrated in the first-person, such works almost always rely upon a convention that attempts to be analogous. The film may begin with a voice-over-visual narration to indicate the first person. Soon, the narration stops and the film gets told from the customary third-person point of view. From time to time, the narrator's voice recurs, reminding us of the first-person narration. It can be seen that such a technique is simply a film convention used to suggest the narrator's voice, but it scarcely can indicate the richness in a successful literary work resulting from the continual voice of the narrator telling the story. Some attempts have been made to make films with a first-person point of view throughout. In these instances the director comes into conflict with one of the main differences between prose and film—film best expresses itself visually. Film theorists have noted that when a voice and an image are of equal strength and are in competition for the viewer's attention, the image dominates. Hence, a film emphasizing verbal narration tends to weaken the visuals in order to make its point. Thus, first-person narrations can be achieved, but the outcome is seldom cinematically satisfactory in the fiction film.

STYLE

In literature, style may be defined as the writer's characteristic use of diction (word choice), grammar and syntax (the way words are arranged in sentences), and figures of speech (hyperbole, metaphor, personification, etc.). For example, Hemingway tends to use a sparse vocabulary, uncomplicated sentence construction, and few figures of speech. On the other hand, Faulkner's vocabulary is quite wide and learned, his sentences are often very complex, and he uses many figures of speech. Obviously, such distinctions are relative. Hemingway's diction is hardly inadequate for his purposes, but with respect to Faulkner's diction, it is sparse. Content influences such stylistic choices in the sense that all fictional elements should serve to reinforce the idea of the work. With this in mind, some readers look upon content, the worlds, situations, and ideas generally expressed by a particular writer, as an important influence upon his style.

V. I. Pudovkin, Eisenstein's colleague, was one of the first theoreticians to note that the shot, the photographed view of the subject, can be considered equal to the word in literature.[55] However, while the ability of film to reproduce concrete words ("bread," for example) is unlimited, cinematic reproduction of abstract words (for

[55]V. I. Pudovkin, "Introduction to the German Edition," *Film Technique and Film Acting*, ed. and trans. Ivor Montagu (New York: Grove Press, Inc., 1970), p. 24. "Introduction" first published in 1928. Most of the book was first published in Russia in 1926.

instance, "faith") is hindered by the same problems expressed in our earlier consideration of metaphor. Thus, if a director were to attempt to capture the diction of a particular work, it would be easier to adapt the concrete diction of Hemingway to the screen than the more abstract diction of Faulkner. For this reason, Hemingway's diction is more "cinematic" than Faulkner's. If a particular writer emphasizes abstract diction in order to produce an artful work, a successful adaptation will prove difficult.

As the word is equal to the shot, the combination of shots in a scene is equal to the sentence. Further, the various methods of transitions from scene to scene produce an effect similar to the paragraph and the chapter of a novel or section of a short story. The various methods of transition from shot to shot and from scene to scene suggest that editing is analogous to grammar, syntax, and paragraph construction in prose fiction. However, while film makes use of an analogous method, prose grammar, syntax, and construction are more precise. For example, while short duration shots often have the effect of sentences, one moving camera shot, in itself, might be a sentence or even a paragraph. Ernest Lindgren describes how the editing process works in film and we can see how this technique is analogous to grammar and syntax:

> The normal method of transition from shot to shot within a scene is by means of a cut which gives the effect of one shot being instantly replaced by the next. The normal method of transition from one scene to another is by means of the mix or dissolve which is always associated with a sense of the passage of time or a break in time. A sequence is normally punctuated by a fade-in at the beginning and a fade-out at the end. The fade may be quick or slow according to the emotional mood of the film at the moment it occurs and to the degree of emphasis which the director desires to give the pause at that particular point.[56]

While this is a description of traditional methods of editing, Lindgren's use of "normal" suggests that this is not always the case. Just as grammar and syntax are changing in modern literature, film

[56]Ernest Lindgren, *The Art of the Film* (New York: Macmillan, 1948), p. 67. Quoted in Bluestone, p. 18.

style in editing is changing also. For example, Bergman's *Persona* (1966) and Bunuel's *Belle De Jour* are almost entirely edited with cuts. Since both films are interested in the interior lives of their characters, rather than the exterior time of the plot, such editing is justified. When we consider the director's editing techniques employed in a filmic adaptation of literature, we should determine how well he uses the possibilities of editing to produce an analogy to the writer's grammar and syntax. Further, if the writer's constructions are traditional, the director should use traditional editing techniques; if the prose work is more experimental, the film should be edited accordingly. However, remember that film, by nature, is presented in the present tense.

The last stylistic element, figures of speech, may be thought of as language used connotatively or language used to express a departure from the literal meaning of the word. Irony, apostrophe, simile, metaphor, and symbol are representative figures of speech. Their use gives the writer a richer method of expression because he is able to describe through analogy or suggest connections in dissimilar things. As noted in the earlier treatment of metaphor, the film is limited in *visually* producing figures of speech. Thus, a writer making extensive use of this element of style would prove difficult to adapt to the screen.

Since the style of a great work of prose fiction is almost always integral to its aesthetic success, we are at the heart of the problem of cinematic adaptations. Film is not able to use analogous methods that satisfactorily reproduce a particular writer's style; hence those films that attempt stylistic adaptations are seldom successful. When they are, it will be found that the writer's style is analogous to the conventions of film style to begin with. However, this may not always be the case in future attempts. It should be remembered that film is an infant art and that it is capable of a much more accurate reproduction of literary style. The experiments in the uses of language by Godard (*One Plus One*, 1968) and the manipulation of time by Resnais (*Last Year at Marienbad*, 1961) suggest the possibilities. In *Literature and Film*, Robert Richardson makes a case for this view:

> The film language, which is the basis of film as a narrative art, seems still to be evolving, and it would be

premature and rash to suggest that it will not eventually develop language with the force, clarity, grace, and subtlety of written language.[57]

TONE

This is the most difficult device to identify in prose. While some suggest that tone is simply the author's attitude toward the material being presented as well as his attitude toward the audience, others choose to include mood, the atmosphere evoked by the material itself. Another way tone could be described would be to say that if theme is *what* a writer says through his work, tone is *how* he intones it. For our purposes, tone will be considered to be the writer's attitude toward the material and his audience (e.g., formal, informal, serious, playful, ironic, honest) as well as the mood or atmosphere found in the work. Tone may be expressed in many ways: diction and imagery are two major methods.

Diction used to present tone is obviously richer in language than in film. With imagery, it is another matter. While imagery has been considered synonymous with certain figures of speech, such as metaphor, simile, symbol, verbal appeals to our five senses are also thought of as imagery. Hence, while film is limited in its ability to adapt the writer's tone found in "visual" figures of speech, it is often able to produce sensory imagery to better effect than language. For instance, an actual sound in a film is more immediately perceived by an audience than onomatopoeia. Feelies, tasties, and smellies, thankfully, remain between the covers of science-fiction.

Tone expressed through mood is often more successful in films than in literature because literature presents its information linearly while film can convey various "messages" simultaneously. For example, a story may begin: "It was a cold, dark, rainy night . . ." and from time to time refer to properties of cold, darkness, and rain for reinforcement. On the other hand, a film could continually present darkness and rain visually, and coldness through certain

[57]Robert Richardson, *Literature and Film* (Bloomington, Ind.: Indiana University Press, 1969), p. 78.

actions of the actors and actresses. The visuals could be accompanied by realistic sounds of rain and appropriate mood music. Simultaneously, plot and action would continue. Thus, the film's analogous methods of producing literary mood are satisfactory and, often, more successful. The key to this success is the flexibility of film in its appeal to our senses. Sounds can be loud or soft, images can be under- or overexposed, the color of the film can be manipulated (even the color of black and white film), lenses can change the quality of the image, film stock of different speeds can be employed. The adapter's task is to select those visual and aural methods at his disposal that produce moods expressed in literature through language.

Rhythm, like diction and imagery, is not primarily a tonal device, but it is often employed in literature and film to that effect. While rhythm may be thought of as an element in poetry rather than prose, fiction is able to produce certain recurrences at regular intervals that either produce the tone of a particular passage or of the entire work. Prose rhythm is created through repetitions of words, recurrences of syntax patterns, and structurings of larger units such as paragraphs or sections. Once an artist sets up the basic tempo of the work, rhythmic changes may then be used as tone changes in given passages. The last paragraph of James Joyce's *The Dead* is a classic example of the use of prose rhythm for tonal effect. Here are the last two sentences of the paragraph:

> It [the snow] lay thickly drifted on the crooked crosses and headstones, on the spears of the little gate, on the barren thorns. His soul swooned slowly as he heard the snow falling faintly through the universe and faintly falling, like the descent of their last end, upon all the living and the dead.[58]

Rhythm in film is central to the concept of editing. Film rhythm may be divided into three types: interior, the quality of the movement within the shot; exterior, the length of time of each shot; and transitional, the length of time between the shots. As in prose, film

[58]James Joyce, *Dubliners*, first printing with corrected text by Robert Scholes (New York: Viking Press, Inc., 1967), pp. 223–224. Reprinted by permission of the publisher.

rhythm may be used to reinforce the material being presented, but it is also a fine method of producing tone.

Film rhythm has one advantage over prose rhythm; editing enables the director to manipulate time in a more immediate fashion than in prose. Interior action can be speeded up (shot at two frames/second) or slowed down (seventy frames/second); the exterior action may be punctuated with cuts, fades, or dissolves; likewise, transitions may be noted through cuts, fades, or dissolves. Since fades and dissolves may be made slowly or quickly, further flexibility results. The visual immediacy of film rhythm may often have a greater impact upon the audience than the methods of punctuation, syntax, or paragraph and section rhythm found in prose. Hence, when diction and imagery produce tone in a given work of prose, the director can sometimes create an analogous tone by placing a greater emphasis upon film rhythm.

THEME

As previously noted, theme is what the author or film-maker says about the subject or the plot. Since all serious prose fiction works have a theme, the film adaptation should attempt to reproduce it. Theme may be expressed through a combination of some or all of the fictional or cinematic elements previously mentioned. This is not to say that any given story or novel will present theme through a balanced use of the elements. Some works express theme through plot and character with stylistic and rhythmic elements used as reinforcements. Others may not be particularly concerned with plot and may, for example, emphasize character and tone to communicate the thematic point of the work. Thus, when evaluating a particular cinematic treatment of a novel or short story, assume that the most successful film adaptation will express the theme of the original work with a similar emphasis on those particular prose elements that the writer found most suitable.

Theme has been the downfall of many serious attempts at film adaptations of novels and short stories for three reasons. Martin C. Battestin notes them in his essay on *Tom Jones:*

> [The script writer's] vision is narrower than Fielding's:
> this is a function partly of the necessary limitations of
> scope in the film, partly of commercial pressures preclud-
> ing "moral seriousness" in a work designed to entertain
> millions, and partly of the different *Weltanshauung*
> [manner of looking at the world] of the twentieth
> century.[59]

Let us examine these reasons in order. The limitations of scope
in film will always be a problem. Naturally, analogy is very important here. If a literary theme is expressed through an elaborate
plot, a wealth of characters, and an elaborate use of figurative language, it would be senseless to call the film a failure because it
could not reproduce the complex theme of the original. However,
it might be possible that the director could carefully select representative parts of the plot, create fewer characters representing
traits, ideas, or positions of many, and substitute setting and tone
for figurative language. In this way, the film would be a successful
adaptation. The other two problems, commercial pressures and
manner of looking at the world, may not be as crucial in the future.
While well-produced film adaptations will always be as costly as
any film done well, the audience for such films is growing. Film
is fast becoming a medium capable of producing works of art as
well as vehicles of entertainment. While many have assumed this
for decades, some since the days of Griffith, we are presently seeing
an acceptance of this fact by the culture. Film as art is being taken
seriously by great masses in our culture and this, in turn, will en-
courage artful products. Such viewers will welcome works of "moral
seriousness" and they will also be able to consider other ways of
looking at the world, the world of the past as well as the present,
with the respect that such alternate views deserve. Naturally, there
will always be "entertainment" films, films made to wile away the
time and reinforce narrow preconceptions, but such shallow works
are to be found in any art form.

While literature and film are separate forms of art, the enter-
prising director will be able to produce an artful adaptation by
employing film techniques that are similar, but not equal to lit-

[59]Battestin, p. 45.

erary techniques. As previously mentioned, analogy is the key. The successful adaptation will not be a copy of the literary work, but a cinematic transformation that captures as much of the spirit and as many of the themes of the original as possible.

Julius Bellone has called the rise of film as an art form since World War II a "film renaissance."[60] This is surely the case, and considerations of film adaptations of literary works have an important place in this renaissance. Through a study of the relationships between literature and film, it is hoped that a knowledge of the similarities and differences between one of our oldest art forms and our youngest will be developed. The result of such an endeavor should be a clearer and more sophisticated understanding of both forms of art.

[60]Julius Bellone, ed., *Renaissance of the Film* (New York: Macmillan, 1970).

THE SHORT STORY

AMBROSE BIERCE

An Occurrence
at Owl Creek Bridge

A man stood upon a railroad bridge in northern Alabama, looking down into the swift water twenty feet below. The man's hands were behind his back, the wrists bound with a cord. A rope closely encircled his neck. It was attached to a stout cross-timber above his head and the slack fell to the level of his knees. Some loose boards laid upon the sleepers supporting the metals of the railway supplied a footing for him and his executioners—two private soldiers of the Federal army, directed by a sergeant who in civil life may have been a deputy sheriff. At a short remove upon the same temporary platform was an officer in the uniform of his rank, armed. He was a captain. A sentinel at each end of the bridge stood with his rifle in the position known as "support," that is to say, vertical in front of the left shoulder, the hammer resting on the forearm thrown straight across the chest—a formal and unnatural position, enforcing an erect carriage of the body. It did not appear to be the duty of these two men to know what was occurring at the center of the bridge; they merely blockaded the two ends of the foot planking that traversed it.

Beyond one of the sentinels nobody was in sight; the railroad ran straight away into a forest for a hundred yards, then, curving, was lost to view. Doubtless there was an outpost farther along. The other bank of the stream was open ground—a gentle acclivity topped with a stockade of vertical tree trunks, loopholed for rifles, with a single embrasure through which protruded the muzzle of a brass cannon commanding the bridge. Midway of the slope between the bridge and fort were the spectators—a single company of infantry in line, at "parade rest," the butts of the rifles on the ground, the barrels inclining slightly backward against the right shoulder, the hands crossed upon the stock. A lieutenant stood at the right of the line, the point of his sword upon the ground, his left hand resting upon his right. Excepting the group of four at the center of the bridge, not a man moved. The company faced the bridge, staring stonily, motionless. The sentinels, facing the banks of the stream, might have been statues to adorn the bridge. The captain stood with folded arms, silent, observing the work of his subordinates, but making no sign. Death is a dignitary who when he comes announced is to be received with formal manifestations of respect, even by those most familiar with him. In the code of military etiquette silence and fixity are forms of deference.

The man who was engaged in being hanged was apparently about thirty-five years of age. He was a civilian, if one might judge from his habit, which was that of a planter. His features were good—a straight nose, firm mouth, broad forehead, from which his long, dark hair was combed straight back, falling behind his ears to the collar of his well-fitting frock coat. He wore a mustache and pointed beard, but no whiskers; his eyes were large and dark gray, and had a kindly expression which one would hardly have expected in one whose neck was in the hemp. Evidently this was no vulgar assassin. The liberal military code makes provision for hanging many kinds of persons, and gentlemen are not excluded.

The preparations being complete, the two private soldiers stepped aside and each drew away the plank upon which he had been standing. The sergeant turned to the captain, saluted and placed himself immediately behind that officer, who in turn moved apart one pace. These movements left the condemned man and the sergeant standing on the two ends of the same plank, which spanned three of the crossties of the bridge. The end upon which the civilian stood almost, but not quite, reached a fourth. This plank had been held in place by the weight of the captain; it was now held by that of the sergeant. At a signal from the former the latter would step aside, the plank would tilt and the condemned man go down between two ties. The arrangement commended itself to his judgment as simple and effective. His face had not been covered nor his eyes bandaged. He looked a moment at his "unsteadfast footing," then let his gaze wander to the swirling water of the stream racing madly beneath his feet. A piece of dancing driftwood caught his attention and his eyes followed it down the current. How slowly it appeared to move! What a sluggish stream!

He closed his eyes in order to fix his last thoughts upon his wife and children. The water, touched to gold by the early sun, the brooding mists under the banks at some distance down the stream, the fort, the soldiers, the piece of drift—all had distracted him. And now he became conscious of a new disturbance. Striking through the thought of his dear ones was a sound which he could neither ignore nor understand, a sharp, distinct, metallic percussion like the stroke of a blacksmith's hammer upon the anvil; it had the same ringing quality. He wondered what it was, and whether immeasurably distant or near by—it seemed both. Its recurrence was regular, but as slow as the tolling of a death knell. He awaited each stroke with impatience and—he knew not why—apprehension. The intervals of silence grew progressively longer; the delays became maddening. With their greater infrequency the sounds increased in strength and sharpness. They hurt his ear like the thrust of a knife; he feared he would shriek. What he heard was the ticking of his watch.

He unclosed his eyes and saw again the water below him. "If I could free my hands," he thought, "I might throw off the noose and spring into the stream. By diving I could evade the bullets and, swimming vigorously, reach the bank, take to the woods and get away home. My home, thank God, is as yet outside their lines; my wife and little ones are still beyond the invader's farthest advance."

As these thoughts, which have here to be set down in words, were flashed into the doomed man's brain rather than evolved from it the captain nodded to the sergeant. The sergeant stepped aside.

Peyton Farquhar was a well-to-do planter, of an old and highly respected Alabama family. Being a slave owner and like other slave owners a politician, he was naturally an original secessionist and ardently devoted to the Southern cause. Circumstances of an imperious nature, which it is unnecessary to relate here, had prevented him from taking service with the gallant army that had fought the disastrous campaigns ending with the fall of Corinth, and he chafed under the inglorious restraint, longing for the release of his energies, the larger life of the soldier, the opportunity for distinction. That opportunity, he felt, would come, as it comes to all in war time. Meanwhile he did what he could. No service was too humble for him to perform in aid of the South, no adventure too perilous for him to undertake if consistent with the character of a civilian who was at heart a soldier, and who in good faith and without too much qualification assented to at least a part of the frankly villainous dictum that all is fair in love and war.

One evening while Farquhar and his wife were sitting on a rustic bench near the entrance to his grounds, a gray-clad soldier rode up to the gate and asked for a drink of water. Mrs. Farquhar was only too happy to serve him with her own white hands. While she was fetching the water her husband approached the dusty horseman and inquired eagerly for news from the front.

"The Yanks are repairing the railroads," said the man, "and are getting ready for another advance. They have reached the Owl Creek bridge, put it in order and built a stockade on the north bank. The commandant has issued an order, which is posted everywhere, declaring that any civilian caught interfering with the railroad, its bridges, tunnels or trains will be summarily hanged. I saw the order."

"How far is it to the Owl Creek bridge?" Farquhar asked.

"About thirty miles."

"Is there no force on this side of the creek?"

"Only a picket post half a mile out, on the railroad, and a single sentinel at this end of the bridge."

"Suppose a man—a civilian and student of hanging—should elude the picket post and perhaps get the better of the sentinel," said Farquhar, smiling, "what could he accomplish?"

The soldier reflected. "I was there a month ago," he replied. "I observed that the flood of last winter had lodged a great quantity of driftwood against the wooden pier at this end of the bridge. It is now dry and would burn like tow."

The lady had now brought the water, which the soldier drank. He thanked her ceremoniously, bowed to her husband and rode away. An hour later, after nightfall, he re-passed the plantation, going northward in the direction from which he had come. He was a Federal scout.

As Peyton Farquhar fell straight downward through the bridge he lost consciousness and was as one already dead. From this state he was awakened—ages later, it seemed to him—by the pain of a sharp pressure up his throat, followed by a sense of suffocation. Keen, poignant agonies seemed to shoot from his neck downward through every fiber of his body and limbs. These pains appeared to flash along well-defined lines of ramification and to beat with an inconceivably rapid periodicity. They seemed like streams of pulsating fire heating him to an intolerable temperature. As to his head, he was conscious of nothing but a feeling of fullness—of congestion. These sensations were unaccompanied by thought. The intellectual part of his nature was already effaced; he had power only to feel, and feeling was torment. He was conscious of motion. Encompassed in a luminous cloud, of which he was now merely the fiery heart, without material substance, he swung through unthinkable arcs of oscillation, like a vast pendulum. Then all at once, with terrible suddenness, the light about him shot upward with the noise of a loud splash; a frightful roaring was in his ears, and all was cold and dark. The power of thought was restored; he knew that the rope had broken and he had fallen into the stream. There was no additional strangulation; the noose about his neck was already suffocating him and kept the water from his lungs. To die of hanging at the bottom of a river!—the idea seemed to him ludicrous. He opened his eyes in the darkness and saw above him a gleam of light, but how distant, how inaccessible! He was still sinking, for the light became fainter and fainter until it was a mere glimmer. Then it began to grow and brighten, and he knew that he was rising toward the surface—knew it with reluctance, for he was now very comfortable. "To he hanged and drowned," he thought, "that is not so bad; but I do not wish to be shot. No; I will not be shot; that is not fair."

He was not conscious of an effort, but a sharp pain in his wrist apprised him that he was trying to free his hands. He gave the struggle his attention, as an idler might observe the feat of a juggler, without interest in the outcome. What splendid effort!

What magnificent, what superhuman strength! Ah, that was a fine endeavor! Bravo! The cord fell away; his arms parted and floated upward, the hands dimly seen on each side in the growing light. He watched them with a new interest as first one and then the other pounced upon the noose at his neck. They tore it away and thrust it fiercely aside, its undulations resembling those of a water snake. "Put it back, put it back!" He thought he shouted these words to his hands, for the undoing of the noose had been succeeded by the direst pang that he had yet experienced. His neck ached horribly; his brain was on fire; his heart, which had been fluttering faintly, gave a great leap, trying to force itself out at his mouth. His whole body was racked and wrenched with an insupportable anguish! But his disobedient hands gave no heed to the command. They beat the water vigorously with quick, downward strokes, forcing him to the surface. He felt his head emerge; his eyes were blinded by the sunlight; his chest expanded convulsively, and with a supreme and crowning agony his lungs engulfed a great draught of air, which instantly he expelled in a shriek!

He was now in full possession of his physical senses. They were, indeed, preternaturally keen and alert. Something in the awful disturbance of his organic system had so exalted and refined them that they made record of things never before perceived. He felt the ripples upon his face and heard their separate sounds as they struck. He looked at the forest on the bank of the stream, saw the individual trees, the leaves and the veining of each leaf—saw the very insects upon them: the locusts, the brilliant-bodied flies, the gray spiders stetching their webs from twig to twig. He noted the prismatic colors in all the dew-drops upon a million blades of grass. The humming of the gnats that danced above the eddies of the stream, the beating of the dragonflies' wings, the strokes of the water spiders' legs, like oars which had lifted their boat—all these made audible music. A fish slid along beneath his eyes and he heard the rush of its body parting the water.

He had come to the surface facing down the stream; in a moment the visible world seemed to wheel slowly round, himself the pivotal point, and he saw the bridge, the fort, the soldiers upon the bridge, the captain, the sergeant, the two privates, his executioners. They were in silhouette against the blue sky. They shouted and gesticulated, pointing at him. The captain had drawn his pistol, but did not fire; the others were unarmed. Their movements were grotesque and horrible, their forms gigantic.

Suddenly he heard a sharp report and something struck the water smartly within a few inches of his head, spattering his face with spray. He heard a second report, and saw one of the sentinels with his rifle at his shoulder, a light cloud of blue smoke rising from the muzzle. The man in the water saw the eye of the man on the bridge gazing into his own through the sights of the rifle. He observed that it was a gray eye and remembered having read that gray eyes were keenest, and that all famous marksmen had them. Nevertheless, this one had missed.

A counter-swirl had caught Farquhar and turned him half round; he was again looking into the forest on the bank opposite the fort. The sound of a clear, high voice in a monotonous sing-song now rang out behind him and came across the water with a distinctness that pierced and subdued all other sounds, even the beating of the ripples in his ears. Although no soldier, he had frequented camps enough to know the dread significance of that deliberate, drawling, aspirated chant; the lieutenant on shore was taking a part in the morning's work. How coldly and pitilessly—with what an even, calm intonation, presaging, and enforcing tranquility in the men—with what accurately measured intervals fell those cruel words:

"Attention, company! . . . Shoulder arms! . . . Ready! . . . Aim! . . . Fire!"

Farquhar dived—dived as deeply as he could. The water roared in his ears like the voice of Niagara, yet he heard the dulled thunder of the volley and, rising again toward the surface, met shining bits of metal, singularly flattened, oscillating slowly downward. Some of them touched him on the face and hands, then fell away, continuing their descent. One lodged between his collar and neck; it was uncomfortably warm and he snatched it out.

As he rose to the surface, gasping for breath, he saw that he had been a long time under water; he was perceptibly farther down stream—nearer to safety. The soldiers had almost finished reloading; the metal ramrods flashed all at once in the sunshine as they were drawn from the barrels, turned in the air, and thrust into their sockets. The two sentinels fired again, independently and ineffectually.

The hunted man saw all this over his shoulder; he was now swimming vigorously with the current. His brain was as energetic as his arms and legs; he thought with the rapidity of lightning.

"The officer," he reasoned, "will not make that martinet's error a second time. It is as easy to dodge a volley as a single shot. He has probably already given the command to fire at will. God help me, I cannot dodge them all."

An appalling splash within two yards of him was followed by a loud, rushing sound, *diminuendo*, which seemed to travel back through the air to the fort and died in an explosion which stirred the very river to its deeps! A rising sheet of water curved over him, fell down upon him, blinded him, strangled him! The cannon had taken a hand in the game. As he shook his head free from the commotion of the smitten water, he heard the deflected shot humming through the air ahead, and in an instant it was cracking and smashing the branches in the forest beyond.

"They will not do that again," he thought; "the next time they will use a charge of grape. I must keep my eye upon the gun; the smoke will apprise me—the report arrives too late; it lags behind the missile. That is a good gun."

Suddenly he felt himself whirled round and round—spinning like a top. The water, the banks, the forest, the now distant bridge, fort and men—all were commingled and blurred. Objects were represented by their colors only; circular horizontal streaks of color—that was all he saw. He had been caught in a vortex and was being whirled on with a velocity of advance and gyration that made him giddy and sick. In a few moments he was flung upon the gravel at the foot of the left bank of the stream—the southern bank—and behind a projecting point which concealed him from his enemies. The sudden arrest of his motion, the abrasion of one of his hands on the gravel, restored him, and he wept with delight. He dug his fingers into the sand, threw it over himself in handfuls and audibly blessed it. It looked like diamonds, rubies, emeralds; he could think of nothing beautiful which it did not resemble. The trees upon the bank were giant garden plants; he noted a definite order in their arrangement, inhaled the fragrance of their blooms. A strange, roseate light shone through the spaces among their trunks and the wind made in their branches the music of Aeolian harps. He had no wish to perfect his escape—was content to remain in that enchanting spot until retaken.

A whiz and rattle of grapeshot among the branches high above his head roused him from his dream. The baffled cannoneer had fired him a random farewell. He sprang to his feet, rushed up the sloping bank, and plunged into the forest.

All that day he traveled, laying his course by the rounding sun. The forest seemed interminable; nowhere did he discover a break in it, not even a woodsman's road. He had not known that he lived in so wild a region. There was something uncanny in the revelation.

By nightfall he was fatigued, footsore, famishing. The thought of his wife and children urged him on. At last he found a road which led him in what he knew to be the right direction. It was as wide and straight as a city street, yet it seemed untraveled. No fields bordered it, no dwelling anywhere. Not so much as the barking of a dog suggested human habitation. The black bodies of the trees formed a straight wall on both sides, terminating on the horizon in a point, like a diagram in a lesson in perspective. Overhead, as he looked up through this rift in the wood, shone great golden stars looking unfamiliar and grouped in strange constellations. He was sure they were arranged in some order which had a secret and malign significance. The wood on either side was full of singular noises, among which—once, twice, and again—he distinctly heard whispers in an unknown tongue.

His neck was in pain and lifting his hand to it he found it horribly swollen. He knew that it had a circle of black where the rope had bruised it. His eyes felt congested; he could no longer close them. His tongue was swollen with thirst; he relieved its fever by thrusting it forward from between his teeth into the cold air. How softly the turf had carpeted the untraveled avenue—he could no longer feel the roadway beneath his feet!

Doubtless, despite his suffering, he had fallen asleep while walking, for now he sees another scene—perhaps he has merely recovered from a delirium. He stands at the gate of his own home.

All is as he left it, and all bright and beautiful in the morning sunshine. He must have traveled the entire night. As he pushes open the gate and passes up the wide white walk, he sees a flutter of female garments; his wife, looking fresh and cool and sweet, steps down from the veranda to meet him. At the bottom of the steps she stands waiting, with a smile of ineffable joy, an attitude of matchless grace and dignity. Ah, how beautiful she is! He springs forward with extended arms. As he is about to clasp her he feels a stunning blow upon the back of the neck; a blinding white light blazes all about him with a sound like the shock of a cannon—them all is darkness and silence!

Peyton Farquhar was dead; his body, with a broken neck, swung gently from side to side beneath the timbers of the Owl Creek bridge.

CRITICISM OF THE SHORT STORY

CLEANTH BROOKS
ROBERT PENN WARREN

From

Understanding Fiction

This story, like "The Necklace" and "The Furnished Room," involves a surprise ending, an ironical turn. The basic question, then, which the story raises is this: Is the surprise ending justified; is it validated by the body of the story; is it, in other words, a mere trick, or is it expressive and functional?

Perhaps the best way to clear the ground for a consideration of this basic question is to raise another question which no doubt will occur to many readers of the story. Is it possible for a man in the last moment of his life to have a vision of the sort which Farquhar has as he falls from the bridge? Many people may be inclined to judge the story in terms of their acceptance or rejection of the psychological realism of this incident. But is it possible to have absolutely convincing evidence on this point? Isn't the fact of the vision something which, in itself, can be accepted without too much strain on the reader's credulity? But there is a much more important consideration to be taken into account. Even if we could arrive at a completely satisfying decision about the psychological realism of the incident, would this fact actually determine the nature of our judgment concerning the story? For reasons to be suggested below, it would not /122/ determine our judgment, and therefore preoccupation with the question is likely to prove a red herring—is likely to distract us from the real problem.

Suppose that we assume for the moment that the incident is psychologically valid; there remain these questions to be answered:

Reprinted from *Understanding Fiction*, 2nd ed. (1959) by permission of Appleton-Century-Crofts, Educational Division, Meredith Corporation.

1. Why does the author withhold from the reader the knowledge that the dying man's vision is merely a vision?

2. Is any revelation of character accomplished thereby?

3. Does the withholding of this information throw any light on the development of a theme for the story?

4. There is an irony generated by the end of the story, but is it a meaningful irony?

What we are leading up to by means of these questions is this:

Fiction is concerned with people, and one of the interests we take in it arises from the presentation of human character and human experience as merely human. Both the common and the uncommon human character or experience interest us, the common because we share in it, and the uncommon because it wakes us to marvel at new possibilities. But it is a great—and not uncommon—error to equate the presentation of character as such, or experience as such, with the specific meaning of fiction. Fiction ... involves a theme, an idea, an interpretation, and attitude toward life developed and embodied in the piece of fiction. Directly or indirectly, through the experience of the characters in the piece of fiction, an evaluation is made—an evaluation which is assumed to have some claim to a general validity. /123/

The plot that depends on some peculiarity of human psychology —as does "An Occurrence at Owl Creek Bridge"—may give us a shock of surprise, but it does not carry a fictional meaning. The peculiar quirk of psychology—the "case study"—must also involve some significant human evaluation, some broadening or deepening of our human attitudes, if it is to be acceptable as fiction. Fiction involves all kinds of human characters and human experiences, common and uncommon, but it is concerned to do more than make a clinical report, medical or psychological. We must keep this firmly in mind. /124/

DISCUSSION QUESTIONS

1. Brooks and Warren pose four questions to which the answer is an implicit but clear "No," and their treatment of the story is largely unsympathetic. Do you

believe that "An Occurrence at Owl Creek Bridge" broadens or deepens our human attitudes? Why or why not?

2. Brooks and Warren refer to the "case study," the clinical report, in their discussion of the story. Examine the language Bierce uses in the story. Does it vary? How would you characterize it? To what extent is the story a "case study"?

"An Occurrence at Owl Creek Bridge"

The "old fashioned" short story often insists on a surprise ending, which is sometimes unconvincing, or mechanical, or both (as in O. Henry's "The Furnished Room"). The modern short story is usually a fragment of life that is in some way striking, perhaps for its psychological accuracy, and the surprise ending is generally scorned. "An Occurrence at Owl Creek Bridge" combines the best features of both types. The surprise ending occurs in the form of an ironical variation on that stalest of endings ". . . and then I woke up." But it is only a surprise ending to the very unsophisticated reader. The pattern of the whiplash reversal in the last sentence occurs in each of the three parts: "The sergeant stepped aside"; "He was a Federal scout"; "Peyton Farquhar was dead . . ." They are signs of a careful craftsman putting details together and placing them in exactly the right place. The final effect is that events which would seem merely melodramatic in the hands of a lesser artist are so restrained and controlled that we observe rather than participate in the action. Bierce is a creator of tapestries: action is slowed down to scene, and structure is the /26/ juxtaposition of tableaux. There are no excessive details, and those given powerfully build up an atmosphere which is far more important to the story than the action. "An Occurrence at Owl Creek Bridge" meets an important test of literary art; namely, a summary of the plot boils away precisely those elements that make the story important. The morbid and pessimistic content of the story, which led Mencken to coin the epithet "Bitter Bierce" and van Wyck

Reprinted from *Insight*, I (1962), 25-28, by permission of Hirsch-graben-Verlag.

Brooks to refer to the author as "a dandified Strindberg," is far less important than the method.

The first section of the story, with its dreadful matter-of-factness in the description of the preparations for the hanging, represents, like the last sentence, the world of harsh reality. The doomed man's wishful thinking is, of course, psychologically true and prepares the reader for the cruelly disappointed dream of the third section.

The second section employs a familiar device of the storyteller and returns to the circumstances leading to the deception and capture of Peyton Farquhar. The sympathy evoked by the description of the main figure is here confirmed. The name, Peyton Farquhar, suggests the aristocrat, and the subsequent description shows him to be a man prepared to make sacrifices for an ideal. His capture by means of a trick and the powerful self-delusion of his imagined escape are thus the more poignant. This story is thus lent a deeper significance in the contrast implied between the North and the South, between hard reality and impractical ideals.

The third section of the story from the time when Farquhar falls from the bridge is marked by a dream-like unreality, beginning with the strange detachment with which Farquhar watches his hands freeing themselves and removing the noose from his neck and rising to a climax at the point where the man in the water sees the eye of the man on the bridge aiming at him through the sights of the rifle. The illusion that Farquhar has really escaped is sustained by the convincing practical detail of the swimmer encountering the hot bullets as he dives up (which was possible with the weapons of the period of the American Civil War) and by the "martinet's error" of the officer in ordering a volley instead of staggered shots. But the awareness that the escape is an illusion is gradually heightened by the fantastic paradisiacal scenery of the stones and trees on the river bank. The scenery becomes increasingly unreal, and the touching effect of wish-fulfillment fantasy reaches a climax in Farquhar's "meeting" with his wife. The last sentence is a return to hard reality, and a confirmation of the reader's worst expectations.

1. *What would be the sophisticated and the unsophisticated ways of reading this story?*

To the unsophisticated reader, the ending comes as a simple surprise. For the reader who demands something more than a surprise ending, there is psychological truth in the wishful thinking of the man about to be executed, a common element of dreams and fantasies. There is irony in the variation on the most hackneyed of surprise endings. At the same time Bierce contrasts two ways of life /27/ and modes of thought which can be roughly summed up under the headings "idealism" and "realism." The story thus has a wide appeal.

2. *Discuss the structure of the story.*

The story goes in medias res, so that the reader's interest is immediately captured by the chief catastrophe. When, in section II, we learn of the event that had led up to the execution, our sympathies are aroused, to give the events in section III their full effect. A great deal would be lost if part II came first. Hemingway is known to have admired this story for its unusual and effective structure; his short story "The Snows of Kilimanjaro" is constructed on exactly the same line: "Both stories open with the situation of impending death, then flash back to explain how the situation came about, and then flash "forward" with the imaginary escape, only to conclude with the objective information that the death has indeed occurred" [Philip Young, *Ernest Hemingway* (Minneapolis, 1959), pp. 30–31].

3. *Do Bierce's views of life appear in the story?*

Bierce's attitude was deeply pessimistic, and in his other writings this pessimism is apt to appear in the form of a raw cynicism. Here the pessimism is more effective because it is implicit in the story. The ardent patriot (who is, however, also a slave-owner) misuses his idealism for purposes of war and is caught and hanged. His wife is "only too happy to serve . . . with her own white hands" the soldier at the gate, who has come to lay a trap for her husband. Farquhar, smiling, calls himself a "student of hanging" and indeed meets with an arrangement that "commended itself to his judgment as simple and effective." He clings to the possibility of escape up to the last moment, but he is ruthlessly aroused from his rosy dreams. The cruelty and pointlessness of war is also illustrated in the story. The distressing event described here is merely "An Incident at Owl Creek Bridge," i.e., a very minor happening at an obscure place. In "A Horseman in the Sky" (another Bierce story) the same element of obscure sacrifice and suffering is emphasized— the hero's shooting of his own father passes almost unnoticed.

4. *How is the prisoner's state of mind indicated?*

We are told of "the swirling water of the stream racing madly beneath his feet." Then the prisoner's attention is caught by a piece of driftwood, and his thoughts are given as "How slowly it appeared to move! What a sluggish stream!" As in a slow-motion picture time almost comes to a standstill when he listens to the ticking of his watch during his last seconds: "He awaited each stroke with impatience and ... apprehension. The intervals of silence grew progressively longer; the delays became maddening." In this way the reader is prepared to accept the dream of escape that the prisoner experiences while falling. The loud noise "like the stroke of a blacksmith's hammer" made by the prisoner's watch moreover shows how preternaturally sensitive he has become. These small incidents indicate that the prisoner's relation to reality is disturbed; that he is capable of being deluded in the way revealed in the last section of the story. /28/

DISCUSSION QUESTIONS

1. Cunliffe claims, "A great deal would be lost if part II came first." Agree or disagree and explain.

2. Cunliffe mentions Bierce's "raw cynicism" and his pessimism. How are they reflected in the story?

3. How does Bierce "emphasize the cruelty and pointlessness of war"?

ERIC SOLOMON

From
"The Bitterness of Battle:
Ambrose Bierce's War Fiction"

It is to be expected that such tightly condensed tales as those of Bierce should demand a certain element of foreshortening. Characters are mere shadows; one action is usually the basis for the tale, and dialogue is held to a bare minimum. Bierce recognizes a basic fact of combat: that in an intense situation the time scheme is often upset; an event that seems to take an eternity may in reality happen in a matter of minutes, and the converse is equally possible.

An outstanding example of this first type of time-manipulation appears in Bierce's most frequently anthologized war story, "An Occurrence at Owl Creek Bridge." Like much of his writing, it is in essence a tour-de-force. The hero, Peyton Farquhar, is about to be hanged from a railroad bridge. Bierce supplies a mournfully slow, cadenced description of the bridge, the soldiers guarding it, the /155/ officer in charge, and the preparations for the hanging. Farquhar becomes conscious of the labored, measured passage of time when he hears a steady stroke sounding for all the world like a death knell; the noise comes from his watch. The trap is sprung, and first the author provides a flashback to Farquhar's previous life, then an increasingly tense narration of his escape from the noose, his rapid flight down the turbulent river, through the bullets of the sentinels and the grape-shot of the artillery. He makes good his escape, returns to his wife—and the last, shocking

Reprinted by permission of the publisher from *The Midwest Quarterly*, V (January, 1964), 147-165. Only pages 155-156 are printed here.

line utterly destroys the carefully wrought illusion. "Peyton Farquhar was dead; his body, with a broken neck, swung gently from side to side beneath the timbers of the Owl Creek Bridge."

The ordering of time, extending the felt experience far beyond the actual number of minutes involved, has become a commonplace in modern fiction. It is important in the context of the war genre because the extension of time to include the past histories and the future hopes of the participants in a military action has been an extremely effective technique for writers who must keep their focus on the battle circumstances in order to sustain the suspense, and yet move away in time and space from the physical restrictions of the battlefield to vary the effects. /156/

DISCUSSION QUESTIONS

1. Provide a character sketch of Peyton Farquhar. What do we know about the protagonist and how do we know it? Is Farquhar, like Bierce's typical characters, only a "shadow"?

2. Why does Bierce extend the time? Is it merely to "include the past histories and the future hopes of the participants in a military action"? Does it have thematic significance?

STUART C. WOODRUFF

From

The Short Stories of Ambrose Bierce

Bierce's most famous story—the best one he ever wrote —is "An Occurrence at Owl Creek Bridge."[1] In its controlling conception and design it resembles most of his war stories; there is the same ironic disparity between reason and imagination, thought and feeling, the same journey through a haunted forest, the dream of happiness and fulfilled desire, followed by the shattering realization that the only possible human condition is one of defeat and death. And once again it is this empirical knowledge which destroys the products of the creative imagination. Literally and symbolically the trap springs shut on Payton Farquhar, as he swings "gently from side to side beneath the timbers of the Owl Creek bridge," his neck broken, his lovely illusion of escape and reunion with his wife a mocking dream. Yet somehow, these familiar elements, so recurrent in Bierce's war fiction, are brought to a kind of final perfection, as if Bierce had found the ideal formula for embodying his despairing insights. "An Occurrence at Owl Creek Bridge" is an outstanding story for several reasons, but chiefly because Bierce entered so fully into the imaginative life of his protagonist. As a result, the story becomes as vivid and convincing, and as charged with compressed symbolic /153/ energy, as Farquhar's hallucination. Paradoxically, the deceptive illusion, which occurs in a matter of seconds, seems more real than the

Reprinted from *The Short Stories of Ambrose Bierce*, by Stuart C. Woodruff, by permission of the University of Pittsburgh Press. ©1964 by the University of Pittsburgh Press.
[1] *Collected Writings*, pp. 9–18.

actual execution, with its statuelike soldiers and officers and the silent intensity of their preparations. For once, at least, Bierce was able to put salt "upon the tail of a dream's elusive spirit."

At the beginning of the story Bierce makes it clear that Farquhar is about as "trapped" as any man can be. Standing in the middle of the bridge with hands tied behind him, a rope about his neck "attached to a stout cross–timber above his head," the condemned spy is surrounded by seven soldiers, two of whom guard either end of the railroad bridge. A short distance away on the river bank stands "a single company of infantry in line." Everything is conducted in eerie silence; the soldiers stare "stonily, motionless," the sentinels "might have been statues to adorn the bridge"; the captain in charge stands "with folded arms, silent." Even the order that drops Farquhar through the railroad ties to his death is given by a slight nod of the head. As he tries "to fix his last thoughts upon his wife and children," Farquhar is conscious of only one sound, a "metallic percussion like the stroke of a blacksmith's hammer upon the anvil." The noise becomes unbearably loud, yet "as slow as the tolling of a death knell"—and that is exactly what it is, for "what he heard was the ticking of his watch." Time runs out on Peyton Farquhar, although in the strange quiet of the scene and the concentrated intensity of his thoughts it appears to cease altogether. The empirical fact is the ticking watch, the destructive life in time; opposed to it is the beautiful dream of escape and freedom, the subjective /154/ reality that would conquer time and all human limitations.

> "If I could free my hands," he thought, "I might throw off the noose and spring into the stream. By diving I could evade the bullets and, swimming vigorously, reach the bank, take the woods and get away home."

Like the fatal ticking of the watch, the stream below is "racing madly," but to Farquhar, "how slowly it appeared to move!" The spy, of course, never reaches its "swirling water." He, not time, hangs suspended over Owl Creek, and in the final image of his body swinging "gently from side to side," like the pendulum on a clock, Bierce finds the ideal symbol of man betrayed by the "pitiless perfection of the divine, eternal plan," trapped by a world that seems to promise so much yet give so little. What Farquhar plunges into is the depths of his own subconscious. His thoughts of escape are not rational plans; they originate in the instinct for self-preservation, but represent as well all instinctive desire, all imaginary dreams that allow man to control his destiny and achieve his goals. As Bierce tells us: "these thoughts . . . were flashed into the doomed man's brain rather than evolved from it," and their compelling power and vitality become the substance of the story. Like that promising song of the mockingbird, however, they are "to sense" only, as reason always reveals.

Instead of juxtaposing the dream and the reality throughout, as he does in many stories, Bierce makes us submit to the power of the irrational imagination by turning Farquhar's innermost thoughts and feelings /155/ into a seemingly real tale of daring escape. Moreover, it is the kind of tale we would *like* to believe because Farquhar himself is such an attractive figure: brave, sensitive, highly intelligent.

> His features were good—a straight nose, firm mouth, broad forehead, from which his long, dark hair was combed straight back, falling behind his ears to the collar of his well-fitting frock-coat. He wore a mustache and pointed beard, but no whiskers; his eyes were large and dark gray, and had a kindly expression which one would hardly have expected in one whose neck was in the hemp. Evidently this was no vulgar assassin.

It is the tragic waste of such a man which engages our sympathies. A wealthy Southerner, Farquhar is made still more sympathetic by the fact that he was deliberately deceived into trying to destroy the Owl Creek Bridge, for which he is executed by the Union soldiers. Before the action of the story, a Federal scout, disguised as a Confederate, had ridden up to Farquhar's plantation and told him of the bridge's importance to the Union cause. Before he rode off as mysteriously as he came, he even hinted that the driftwood caught against its pilings "would burn like tow." Thus Farquhar is doomed from the beginning, the idea of helping the South planted in his mind by an enemy who, presumably, intends to confiscate Farquhar's property once he has been hanged as a spy. His act, in turn, was motivated by a "longing for the release of his energies, the larger life of the soldier, the opportunity for distinction."

Once we plunge with Farquhar into the timeless realm of the subconscious, the story becomes simultaneously /156/ as real, and as unreal, as all our dreams. Bierce handles this ambiguity with flaw-less tact and balances the entire story on the polarities of our response. Reading quickly or casually, one is easily convinced that Farquhar has, in fact, escaped, and the ending comes as a stunning shock. Reading deliberately—that is, with the mind alert for the rational "facts" of the situation—one realizes that it is only a vivid dream. Somehow the reader is made to participate in the split between imagination and reason, to *feel* that the escape is real while he *knows* that it is not. What we want from the story and what we get from it are two different things; like Farquhar, we hang suspended between two worlds. What makes the whole affair so apparently real are the "sensations" of the spy—the "sense of suffocation," "of congestion," the desperate need of air, the "roaring" of the water in his ears as he struggles to free his hands and dislodge the rope. All this, however, is imagined in the few seconds consumed by his drop: "The intellectual part of his nature was already effaced; he had power only to feel, and feeling was torment." Farquhar is the typical Bierce hero, victim of acute sensations and the tricks they play on him. Some of the sensations suggest the actual circumstances while simultaneously reinforcing the illusion. For example, Farquhar, imagining himself weightless in the water, feels that he is swinging "through unthinkable arcs of oscillation, like a vast pendulum," that he is "without material substance," that "all was cold and dark."

All of the spy's "physical senses" are "preternaturally keen and alert" and give his experiences a deceptive /157/ concreteness which, upon close inspection, is seen to be impossible. Breaking the surface of the water, his eyes "blinded by the sunlight," Farquhar can see the trees of the forest, "the leaves and the veining of each leaf," the "prismatic colors in all the dewdrops upon a million blades of grass." Even the "strokes of the water-spiders' legs" make "audible music" "like oars which had lifted their boat." Yet this very concreteness gives the escape an authentic ring of truth. Excited soldiers, silhouetted "against the blue sky," shout and gesticulate,

Farquhar is spun and buffeted by the current, shots splatter all around him and he dives "as deeply as he could." As he rises for air he meets "shining bits of meal, singularly flattened, oscillating slowly downward." When one drops down his collar "it was uncomfortably warm and he snatched it out." It is this kind of specific detail that keeps persuading the reader that perhaps the impossible has happened, that the rope did break and that soon Farquhar will be safe in the forest. Whirled downstream, Farquhar finds himself momentarily hidden "behind a projecting point which concealed him from his enemies." He blesses the sand in gratitude for his escape. The world is transfigured, a new Eden in which the trees "were giant garden plants," the forest suffused in "a strange roseate light," filled with "the music of aeolian harps." Only the "whiz and rattle of grapeshot" makes him leave this "enchanting spot." Springing to his feet, Farquhar "plunged into the forest."

What was an Eden by day becomes at night something weirdly ambiguous, a nightmare of flight rather than a dream of safety. As in "A Tough Tussle," the /158/ forest symbolizes the haunted mind of its occupant, victimized by the irrational imagination and the contents it throws up from the depths of the subconscious. Its possibilities are endless: "The forest seemed interminable; nowhere did he discover a break it it. . . . He had not known that he lived in so wild a region. There was something uncanny in the revelation." With a dream's irrational logic, a road suddenly materializes. It is "untraveled," yet runs "wide and straight as a city street" through the forest. The frightening thing about this seeming avenue of escape is that it leads nowhere—it terminates "on the horizon in a point, like a diagram in a lesson in perspective." Above his head Farquhar sees "strange constellations" and is certain they are "arranged in some order which had a secret and malign significance." Instead of being assured of his safety, he appears to doubt the validity of his own dream, as if he were now on the threshold of consciousness. He is haunted by ambiguous sensations, poised between the terror of impending death and the seductive dream of reunion with his family.

"An Occurrence at Owl Creek Bridge" is itself a "lesson in perspective," simultaneously scaled to the life in time and the life where time does not exist, to the appearance of things and to the reality of things. As he walks down the eerie road, the fugitive from destructive realities is conscious that his neck is "horribly swollen." To relieve his parched tongue, he thrust it into the cool night air. The drop has taken place; Farquhar is at the end of his rope. Yet he is still in the haunted forest of acute sensation: "how softly the turf had carpeted the untraveled avenue—he could /159/ no longer feel the roadway beneath his feet!" In the split second before his neck is broken, "he stands at the gate of his own home." To convey the intensity of this last sensation—of desire fulfilled— Bierce shifts to the historical present as he describes Farquhar's wife, "fresh and cool and sweet," descending the veranda steps. "At the bottom of the steps she stands waiting, with a smile of ineffable joy, an attitude of matchless grace and dignity." But she is only the beautiful dream of happiness that always eludes us. This was the lesson Haïta the shepherd learned. Farquhar learns it now, for as he "springs forward with extended arms" the vision disappears, obliterated by the cracking neck bone, the "darkness and silence."

This is the way it must always end in Bierce's fiction. The dreamer is "awakened" to a real world of futility and death, just as Bierce, who dreamed of romantic exciting experience in his haunted forest, awoke to the reductive realities of the Gilded Age and his limitations as an artist. Like Peyton Farquhar, Bierce longed "for the release of his energies, the large life of the soldier, the opportunity for distinction." He became, like Farquhar, "a civilian who was at heart a soldier." In a poem called "My Day of Life,"[2] Bierce reviews the rich experience that comes to him in dreams at daybreak:

> And, O I've dreamed so many things!
>   One hardly can unravel
> The tangled web of visionings
> That slumber-of-the-morning brings:
>   Play, study, work and travel; /160/
>
> The love of women (mostly those
>   Were fairest that were newest);
> Hard knocks from friends and other foes:

Compacts with men (my memory shows
   The deadest are the truest);

War—what a hero I became
   By merely dreaming battle!
Athwart the field of letters, Fame
Blared through the brass my weary name
   With an ominous death-rattle.

Such an eternity of thought
   Within a minute's fraction!
Such phantoms out of nothing wrought,
And fading suddenly to naught
   As I awake to action!

They scamper each into its hole,
   These dreams of my begetting.
They've had their moment; take, my soul,
Thy day of life. . . . Gods! this is droll—
   That thieving sun is setting![3]

If the next-to-last stanza is the unwritten epigraph of "An Occurrence at Owl Creek Bridge," the poem itself describes the pattern of Bierce's fiction as a whole, for it fuses the knowledge and the dream into a bitter awareness of "phantoms out of nothing wrought."

"We are all," Bierce remarked, "dominated by our imaginations and our views are creatures of our viewpoints."[4] Bierce's own views were always precariously balanced between the polarities of his response to art and to life. One viewpoint saw imagination as man's greatest endowment; another saw it as the curse of illusions painfully exposed. The romantic called for the romance "that owes no allegiance to the God of /161/ Things as They Are"; the cynical realist prided himself on being "devoid of all delusions." Such a dual conception determines the form of almost every story Bierce wrote and the obsessive nature of his irony. Only in the war tales could he give his divided sensibility a coherent form and meaning, but that is all he could do. "An Occurrence at Owl Creek Bridge"

---

[3] Ibid. Significantly, these dreams occur at sunrise—that is, at the dawn of life, the period of youth and forward-looking expectations.
[4] "Fin de Siècle," Works, IX, p. 139.

turns his dilemma into a work of art by making the deceptive imagination more "real" than its final defeat; few other stories approach its excellence. . . . /162/

DISCUSSION QUESTIONS

1. Woodruff reprints "My Day of Life," a Bierce poem, and comments in passing on its relation to Bierce's short story. Explain in detail how the poem relates to the story.

2. Woodruff comments on the dichotomy between reality and illusion, the real world and the dream. How "realistically" are the different parts of the story treated? In terms of the story, what constitutes "realism"?

THOMAS L. ERSKINE

Language and Theme in
"An Occurrence
at Owl Creek Bridge"

Although "An Occurrence at Owl Creek Bridge" is commonly regarded as Ambrose Bierce's best and most famous short story, its "surprise ending" is not universally admired. Seeing obvious comparisons to O. Henry's "The Furnished Room," Cleanth Brooks and Robert Penn Warren regard the ironic turn of events as an unjustified "trick," existing for its own sake and totally without what they call "fictional meaning."[1] W. Gordon Cunliffe also notes the superficial resemblance between the stories by Bierce and O. Henry, but while he describes the O. Henry ending as unconvincing and mechanical, he praises Bierce's ending and observes that the surprise ending is a "surprise" only to the unsophisticated reader.[2] In fact, Bierce skillfully and unobtrusively prepares us for the ironic end of the story by using "whiplash reversals" at the end of each part of the story.[3] Cunliffe's perceptive and informative comments about ironic anticipations point us to a larger and more inclusive matter, Bierce's manipulation of time and audience through language. Bierce has it both ways, then: he seduces us into believing in the "reality" of Farquhar's escape and simultaneously leaves us all the clues we need to know that the escape is unreal.

[1] *Understanding Fiction*, 2nd ed. (New York: Appleton-Century-Crofts, 1959), pp. 122–3.
[2] "An Occurence at Owl Creek Bridge," in *Insight* I (1962), 26.
[3] Ibid.

In the first few paragraphs of Part One of his short story, Bierce writes from the strictly objective point of view of a detached, somewhat aloof, mildly curious spectator.[4] After describing the man on the bridge, Bierce moves back until his field of vision slowly enlarges, and he then describes the Federal soldiers and the setting—the river, the railroad, the forests. By "tracking back" Bierce effectively distances us from the situation and, more importantly, places Farquhar in a context which depersonalizes him and emphasizes the theme of insignificant man at the mercy of impersonal institutions. In order to convey the impersonality, Bierce writes scientifically, not poetically; that is, he avoids figurative language and uses in its stead denotative diction. For the most part, in the first four paragraphs we are "outside" Farquhar and see only the surface detail and ritual. Bierce does not editorialize about his material, but describes it in matter-of-fact fashion: the sentences are loose rather than periodic; short rather than long; and a bit choppy rather than coherent. In addition to the style, which incidentally alienates the reader and turns him against the "military code," Bierce's lengthy definitions of technical terms ("support," "parade rest") and his apparent neglect of Farquhar reflect the dominance of code and institution over man. It is not that institutions are hostile to man, but that they are marvelously indifferent to him. This naturalistic view, one Bierce shared with Stephen Crane, is reflected through imagery: "The company faced the bridge, staring *stonily* [my italics], motionless. The sentinels, facing the banks of the stream, might have been *statues* [my italics] to adorn the bridge." The figurative language that Bierce uses neither animates nor personifies inanimate things, but renders the living inanimate. In effect, Bierce enlists our sympathy for Farquhar not by presenting him in depth, but by depicting a mechanical and destructive force that makes man appear insignificant.

Even when he describes Farquhar (paragraph 3), Bierce avoids value judgments and, for the most part, confines himself to

---

[4] Eric Solomon terms the opening of the story a "mournfully slow, cadenced description of the bridge . . ." ["The Bitterness of Battle," in *The Midwest Quarterly* V (1964), 1551, but Cunliffe shares with me the belief that the language is characterized by "dreadful matter-of-factness" (p. 27).

Farquhar's physical appearance. Throughout the paragraph Bierce plays down his knowledge of the facts: "apparently," "if one might judge," "evidently." As Part Two makes clear, Bierce has the answers, but they would be out of place here since he wants to stress the effect of the "liberal military code." In the fourth hanging; it reads like "How To" instructions with short, choppy sentences, step-by-step chronological order—only the numbers are missing. At this point Bierce changes his focus from the procedure to the man, and we are quickly within Farquhar, who notices a piece of "dancing driftwood." Because it is the first example of personification, the phrase ties Farquhar to life and contrasts him with soldiers, who are "stony," "statues."

Bierce devotes the following paragraph exclusively to Farquhar and the change in style is even more pronounced: there are several similes, personification ("brooding mists") and poetic diction ("touched to gold by the early sun"); the sentences are longer and varied. (There are periodic sentences for the first time in the story, and the use of dashes slows the pace.) Thus, Bierce early establishes two writing styles: a poetic one identified with Farquhar, and a mechanical one identified with the reality of war.

Throughout the story the two writing styles reflect the clash between Farquhar's imaginative and idealistic view of life and the persistent ironic reminders of the real world. In Part One two clashes anticipate the final irony. The "new disturbance," which is like a "blacksmith's hammer" and a "death knell" to the imaginative Farquhar, is *really* the ticking of his watch; and the heroic fantasy about an escape ends abruptly with Bierce's, "The sergeant stepped aside." By the end of Part One, Bierce has characterized through language the individual and the system and has twice shown us ironic reality undercutting imaginative fantasies.

Part One primarily concerns the system; Part Two deals with Farquhar's background. A careful reading of the first paragraph explains in part Farquhar's fantasy and intensifies the clash between the harsh reality of war and imaginative, romantic ideals of man. Like Henry Fleming, the protagonist of Crane's *The Red Badge of Courage*, Farquhar has unrealistic ideas about the war: "...and he chafed under the inglorious restraint, longing for the release of his energies, the larger life of the soldier, the opportunity for distinction." Though a civilian, Farquhar considers himself a soldier, though his behavior differs radically from that of the *real* soldiers of Part One. Like a "good soldier," he assents to the cliché that "all is fair in love and war," and he thereby ironically seals his own doom. As in Part One, Part Two ends with the ironic destruction of a successful dream: Farquhar believes that he can burn the bridge, but his informant "was a Federal scout." It is significant that the last paragraph of Part Two is written straightforwardly, whereas the first paragraph is written poetically. Part Two, then, furthers our sympathetic identification with Farquhar, who is a romantic dreamer and the victim of a betrayal.

After the exposition of Part Two Bierce returns to the hanging. In recounting Farquhar's escape, Bierce deliberately avoids the mechanical prose style of Part One. We are inside Farquhar and see from his eyes. As a result, Part Three tends toward the poetic, the lyrical, the evocative—in short, an imaginative style and diction. Pains become "streams of pulsating fire"; the noose, a water snake; the water, the "voice of Niagra." This is not, as we have seen, the language of the "real," but we ignore the clues because the language is so compelling and so seductive.

"Encompassed in a luminous cloud, of which he was merely the fiery heart, without material substance, he swung through unthinkable arcs of oscillation, like a vast pendulum." This mystical passage draws us into Farquhar's world, and by the end of the paragraph we *believe*. Yet the passage also relates to time, one of the story's prime concerns. As Stuart C. Woodruff points out, at the end of the story Farquhar's body swings like the pendulum of a clock; man cannot escape time.[5] In the passage above Bierce poetically and mystically suggests extraterrestrial time, perhaps eternity, but the real is the hanging body caught in time.

Early in the story Farquhar dreams of escape, and we discover in Part Two that he dreams of heroic grandeur in war. We should not be taken in, then, by the following:

[5] *The Short Stories of Ambrose Bierce* (Pittsburgh: University of Pittsburgh Press, 1964), p. 154.

> He gave the struggle his attention, as an idler might observe the feat of a juggler, without interest in the outcome. What splendid effort! What magnificent strength! Ah, that was a fine endeavor! Bravo!

The passage should suggest unreality to us: thought and feeling are divorced, and Farquhar is fragmented; he sees a juggler, an entertainer, an actor playing at reality; and the language calls to mind Farquhar's earlier dreams, all of which have been destroyed.

As Farquhar gains full possession of his physical senses, he finds that they are "preternaturally keen and alert," and most readers accept the outrageous hyperbole that follows. From the river Farquhar sees "the veining of each leaf" and the insects on those leaves, and he hears the "rush" of a fish's body. The paragraph works because it is lyrical and beautiful. However, in our admiration for such touches as the simile between the stokes of the water spiders' legs and the oars of a boat we should devote more attention to some of the things which Farquhar sees: in the forest he sees locusts, flies, and spiders; in the stream he sees gnats, dragonflies, and water spiders. The two sequences, which are roughly parallel, suggest destruction, entrapment, and death and also comment ironically on Farquhar's escape. In a similar vein, Farquhar becomes "the pivotal point" around which the world revolves, and we do not so much see him as we see things, as we move with him, from his viewpoint. As a result, we see the eye of the man with the rifle, and we find the forms of the soldiers gigantic, but without the identification we would be struck by the absurdity of such sights. Even the mechanized sounds of war are romanticized and almost muted by Bierce's style. Using alliteration ("dread significance of that deliberate, drawling"), parallelism ("with what" phrases), and dashes, Bierce renders the material of Part One powerless.

When he finally reaches the shore, Farquhar finds an Eden, a world totally unrealistic and obviously symbolic: the sand looks like jewels; the trees are "giant garden plants" (and Bierce's switch from simile to metaphor indicates the symbolic import of the place); there is a "strange roseate light" and, romantically, "the music of Aeolian harps; and the spot is "enchanting." At this point in his odyssey Farquhar has retreated in time and is further than ever from the sober facts of reality. Interestingly, Bierce nowhere hints that the Eden is unreal; on the contrary, Farquhar is "restored" when he is washed up on shore. But, true to his technique, Bierce abruptly "restores" us to reality: the grapeshot "roused him from his dream." In a sense, then, Bierce once again proves that one can neither distort time nor forsake the real for the dream.

After fleeing from the Eden, Farquhar finds himself in an "interminable" (which reflects upon the theme of disjointed time) forest. As Stuart C. Woodruff has pointed out, the dream of safety (which, ironically, lies in the past, rather than in the future) is succeeded by "a nightmare of flight," and the forest becomes "weirdly ambiguous."[6] The road he finds is "as wide and straight as a city street," but it "seemed untraveled." Moreover, the "black bodies" (personifying animate things) of trees ironically create a "wall," which is inanimate. What would strike us as mixed metaphor in an amateur become a means of creating ambiguity and irony in the hands of a craftsman. Certainly this is not a literal forest, but a symbolic, even allegorical, one which suggests, like Dante's "Wood of Error," the tangled world through which Everyman must pass. The description of the road is reminiscent of Crane: man is alone, walled in and with no hope of escape; the universe seems "malign," and the only noises are "whispers in an unknown tongue."[7] In terms of language, this part of the story is furthest from the mechanical, scientific style of Part One. Bierce uses alliteration ("fatigued, footsore, famishing"), paradox (the untraveled city street), simile, and even suggestions of allegory. We are clearly in an unreal world, and we would know it, were it not that we are Farquhar by this point in the story. We ignore the facts: Farquhar *feels* pain (Bierce describes Farquhar's "swollen neck," his "congested" eyes, his swollen tongue), but he cannot feel the roadway he walks on. There is no substance to Farquhar's escape.

[6] Ibid., p. 168.
[7] Crane uses similar themes throughout his poetry, and the last image recalls the end of "An Experiment in Misery."

As he has done earlier in the story, Bierce suggests that at least part of his story is unreal: just as Farquhar wakes from his dream Eden, he now believes that he has been "asleep," hence dreaming, or that he has "merely recovered from a delirium." Yet we still believe in the reality of his escape. Unobtrusively Bierce adds to the "reality" of the escape by shifting tenses from past to present. We are there; we have succeeded in going home again. Even when Farquhar feels the "stunning blow to the back of the neck," we are a bit confused and probably miss the hint ("like the shock of a cannon") Bierce provides. Bierce's facts are not apparent until the last paragraph of the story, where he again returns to the sparse, scientific prose of Part One. The facts, not the dreams, have the last word.

A careful reading of the story, then, absolves Bierce of the implicit charges leveled against him by Brooks and Warren. I think it is perfectly clear that the ending is not an unjustified "trick," and, further, that the four questions they ask regarding the story must be answered affirmatively.[8] Through language Bierce stresses the clash between reality and vision; he shows us an idealistic dreamer at odds with a system; he constantly keeps the theme of time before the reader and ties the end to that theme; and his ironic ending is part of a larger ironic pattern that permeates the work. If there is a "trick," it is not played on the reader, but on Man—Man, the romantic, impractical dreamer in a mutable and real world.

[8] *Understanding Fiction*, p. 123.

JOHN KENNY CRANE

From

"Crossing the Bar Twice: Post Mortem Consciousness in Bierce, Hemingway, and Golding"

In 1891 Ambrose Bierce, in a story entitled "An Occurrence at Owl Creek Bridge," developed a technique that later scholars have chosen to call "post-mortem consciousness." This refers to any story in which a dying man seems to experience an extended series of sensations *after* death has ostensibly overcome him. Since Bierce only two other writers of stature have tried it. Ernest Hemingway included it with innovations in "The Snows of Kilimanjaro" (1936), and William Golding further explored the possibilities of the device in his novella *Pincher Martin* (1956)....

Bierce, obviously most interested in the technique *per se*, attributes the moment of post-mortem consciousness to various unfulfilled desires of the human heart—his story involves a man about to be hanged who fears for the welfare of his family.

"Post-mortem consciousness" is actually a misnomer. It does not mean, as the term implies, that the character is aware of reality even after he has died. More accurately and less literally, post-mortem consciousness connotes a very definite attempt made by the dying self in the last second *before* death consumes it, but also in the first second *after* death can possibly be averted, to im-

Reprinted from *Studies in Short Fiction*, VI (1969), 361-376. Only pages 361-365 are reprinted here.

pose its own rule upon the universal order in place of the inevitable fate (death) that is coming to pass. Rather /361/ than being consciousness *after* death, it is a hypersensitive consciousness *in* the moment of death. It is a surging momentary struggle to realize the will of the self despite the impossibility and finality of the situation.

All three writers face problems of biology and psychology in such a literary endeavor—who, after all, knows what it is like to die? Does death merely resemble the last flicker of a fading candle or is it truly the phenomenal occurrence that man, as a reluctantly mortal being, always secretly assumes it will and ought to be? Bierce, Hemingway, and Golding favor the latter possibility, and they all display in their rendering of death the same four phases of post-mortem consciousness. Phase I—the dying man, still very much alive, notices time slowing down as the moment of extinction approaches. This of course is a psychological lie. Phase II—the slowing of the time brings on extreme hypersensitivity—elements of life the dying man had previously found ordinary, passive, or unintelligible suddenly assume fantastic importance. Phase III —the dying man takes this new sense data and imposes a *temporary reality* upon the universe. He quickly discards the harsh fact of extinction in favor of a more ideal (and apparently more real) turn of events. Phase IV—at the very moment this fantastic experience seems to the endurer most clear, most real, and most ultimately satisfying, he dies. . . .

I

As Philip Young points out in his book on Hemingway,[1] we must remember, while admiring the technical precision of "The Snows of Kilimanjaro," that Bierce did it first. Without "An Occurrence at Owl Creek Bridge" Hemingways's story probably would not exist. Thus, if we find Bierce's work pale in its light and, especially, in that of the more extensive attempt by Golding, we /362/ can easily forgive him. Bierce had an original idea and apparently was content to employ a very simple plot in order to perfect the technique itself. Peyton Farquhar, a Southern sympathizer

[1] *Ernest Hemingway: A Reconsideration* (University Park, Pa., 1966), p. 197.

during the Civil War, is introduced standing on a bridge, about to be hanged for treason by a contingent of Union soldiers. As he awaits the hanging, he reflects sentimentally upon his home and family and, of course, wishes he were there and not here. As he drops toward the river at the second of execution, the rope breaks; and, after untying his hands beneath the water, he swims wildly downstream with soldiers shooting from all sides. When he is finally out of range he climbs ashore and runs for his house. As he is about to embrace his wife, bang!—the rope breaks his neck. Farquhar and the reader have both been fooled. It is this narrative technique that fascinates both Hemingway and Golding; the plot, though, they both reject as unreal and overly simple.

It is, of course, the blatant sentimentality that mars the story. Early in the tale Bierce defines Death as "a dignitary ... to be received with formal manifestations of respect" and Farquhar seems to think the greatest formal sacrifice he is making to Death is the severing of the close bond between him and his family. He has no thoughts whatsoever about the Southern cause for which he is dying or the natural bitterness one ought to feel against the conniver who trapped him into his present predicament. As Farquhar waits to be hanged, Bierce begins to develop the "swollen moment." The condemned man, attempting to concentrate for one last minute on his family, is suddenly distracted:

> ... Striking through the thought of his dear ones was a sound which he could neither ignore nor understand, a sharp, distinct, metallic percussion like the stroke of a blacksmith's hammer upon the anvil; it had the same ringing quality. He wondered what it was and whether immeasurably distant or near by—it seemed both. Its recurrence was regular, but as slow as the tolling of a death knell. He awaited each stroke with impatience and—he knew not why—apprehension. The intervals of silence grew progressively longer; the delays became maddening. With their greater infrequency the sounds increased in strength and sharpness. They hurt his ear like the thrust of a knife; he feared he would shriek. What he heard was the ticking of his watch.

In terms of the four phases of the post-mortem consciousness process (swollen moment, hypersensitivity, temporary reality, /363/ death), notice first of all that the ticking is initially regular, but later the intervals between each tick grow progressively longer. The delays become maddening. Surely his watch is not slowing down—his personal time is.[2] The moments are already expanding in preparation for the swollen moment between the initiation of his few-foot descent through the boards and the second when the knot of the rope breaks his neck. But observe also the onset of hypersensitivity; the ticking resembles a blacksmith beating an anvil and eventually seems like the sound of a church bell slicing with incisive sharpness into his eardrum. When the sergeant steps aside and Farquhar is dropped straight down towards the water, the hanged man feels a pain in his neck, a sense of suffocation, a congestion in his throat, a roaring of blood in his ears, and his whole body "swinging like a vast pendulum." In one quick second, he plunged, choked, swung, and died. But what the story involves is the moment between the swing and death.

While his senses still remain hyperactive, he *imagines* that the rope has broken, that he has plunged into the river, that he has untied his hands, and that he is swimming furiously downstream under the fire of the soldiers on the shore. With this series of imaginings, Phase III of the process begins. Farquhar is being propelled downstream by the instincts of his heart—the shooting becomes a mere technicality in the whole event—the man is driven by the need for his family. Nothing else, including the Southern cause that got him into the mess, is even worth considering. Behaving preternaturally, his senses direct the elimination of every hindrance—he even makes slide rule calculations on the speed of cannon shells and knows just when to duck. After what seems like a long time, he finds himself running through the wilderness around his home. The wildness (which he remarks he never noticed before) of the area through which he is fleeing contrasts vividly with his impressions of the brightness and beauty of his

[2] Personal time, according to Bergson, Poulet and others, is time as experienced by a given individual as opposed to time regulated by a clock.

home and the sweetness, grace, and dignity of his wife. Thus, for a brief flash (which does not seem brief at all to Farquhar's psyche), he sees things as they should have been—he has imposed a *temporary reality*, the desires of his heart, upon the true reality of his hanging within the confines of the swollen moment of his post-mortem consciousness. As he is about to embrace his wife, the knot of the noose deals him a stunning blow on the back of his neck. "Peyton Farquhar was dead, his body . . . swung /364/ gently from side to side beneath the timbers of Owl Creek Bridge."

This is post-mortem consciousness in its least complicated form —the slowing of time, the hypersensitivity, the vision of temporary reality, and death. In theme the story is consistent, as Mr. Woodruff points out,[3] with most of Bierce's other work. It has vividly, though sentimentally, portrayed a world of futility and death that forever dooms man's finer instincts to be illusions and no more. This theme rather than anything else was to have been the essence of the story; but posterity has ignored the theme in favor of this original and stunning new technique. /365/

DISCUSSION QUESTIONS

1. Crane writes that the story is marred by "blatant sentimentality," yet other critics find that the story illustrates Bierce's cynicism and pessimism. Are the two views contradictory? Support your answer. If the story contains both irony and sentimentality, what does Bierce achieve? What does the presence of irony and sentimentality add to the story?

2. Crane believes that in the "third stage" the will imposes its own rules on reality. How well does Crane's view account for the nightmarish forest?

[3] Stuart C. Woodruff, *The Short Stories of Ambrose Bierce: A Study in Polarity* (Pittsburgh, 1964), pp. 153–163.

THE FILMS

Introduction to
the Shot Analysis

The *shot analysis* is an interpretive transcript of a film based on its final edited version as seen by the theater audience. It is superior to the *shooting script* of the film in that it describes the finished work rather than the filmmaker's projected plans for the finished work. Naturally, no verbal description can actually duplicate the experience of seeing the film, but the shot analysis allows one to carefully analyze the film after having seen it. Film critics sometimes err in their factual description of a particular film, and such errors often destroy their carefully reasoned interpretation; the shot analysis allows one to reconsider certain visual constructs and key speeches when repeated screenings of the film would not be practical. Finally, many films are so carefully formed and so densely textured that the shot analysis enables the viewer to investigate directorial subtleties that may not be apparent, even after a number of screenings of the film. For all of these reasons, the shot analysis must verbally record the sound, the visuals, and the structuring of the film in a meaningful way, and this is made possible through a kind of descriptive shorthand.

SHOT

A shot is a reproduction of an image from the time the camera starts to the time it stops. It may be shortened by eliminating the beginning and/or end of the resulting strip of film. In the shot analysis, each shot is numbered and the designated shot number precedes the description. When a given shot is a duplication of one seen earlier, this is noted (34 (=18)). At the end of each shot description duration is given in seconds or rough fractions of seconds (10). In the shot analysis of "The Bridge," duration is sometimes given in terms of the number of frames per shot when such information seems meaningful.

KINDS of SHOTS

Shots are conventionally described as *long* (LS), *medium* (MS), or *close-up* (CU). The long shot would show the bodies of one or more people, the medium shot would show one or more people, usually from the waist up, the close-up would show the head and shoulders of one person. On occasion, these shots are described as being *medium* (M) or *extreme* (E). Thus, if a shot presents us with a panoramic view of nature or a view of a person's eyes, the following descriptions would be appropriate: ELS, ECU. Another shot could show a person from the chest up: MCU.

SHOT TRANSITIONS

Shots are joined or edited together in various ways, usually by cuts. Here, one image is immediately replaced by another. Since the *cut* is the usual method of shot transition, it is not noted in the shot analysis. Fades and dissolves are noted as they occur. A *fade-in* transition begins with a black screen, gradually becoming light until the next shot is seen. A *fade-out* transition gradually darkens the scene until the screen is black. When a transition is termed a *dissolve*, one shot is seen to fade out while the next shot fades in. During the midpoint of such a transition, the two shots can be seen as superimpositions. While the duration of the cut is always uniform, the duration of fades and dissolves is not. Both "The Bridge" and "An Occurrence at Owl Creek Bridge" have shots in which images are superimposed over other images. When these superimpositions appear or disappear, they are noted as fading in or fading out over the previously established image. Several shots in "The Bridge" consist of *iris wipes*. In the basic *wipe* transition, a line moves across the screen, replacing an old image with a new image as it goes. The *iris* effect is created by masking the frame in such a way that the image begins as a pinpoint or small section of the frame and, as the non-masked area is gradually enlarged, proceeds to fill the frame (*iris-in*) or by masking the frame by beginning with a full-frame shot and ending up with a pinpoint or small portion image (*iris-out*). In most iris transitions, the frame begins or ends in darkness; however, in the iris wipe shot, an old image is replaced with a new image as the iris effect is employed.

CAMERA MOVEMENT

The camera may be moved within a shot in various ways. It may *pan* (move horizontally on a fixed axis) *tilt* (move vertically on a fixed axis), or do both at the same time. In the shot analysis this latter movement is called a *diagonal*. The cameraman may carry out these movements at any speed he desires. Very fast movement is termed a *zip*. Other camera movement may be achieved by bodily moving the camera as well as its axis. This is called a *track*, since it was usually carried out in the early days of the film by actually placing the camera on tracks. At present, however, tracking is most often done by placing the camera and its axis on a rubber-tired vehicle. A tracking shot may be said to be *forward*, *backward*, *vertical*, *lateral*, or *diagonal*. Some use the term *travel* to indicate that the tracking shot is moving at a different speed than the object being photographed. A tracking shot of a fixed object is sometimes called a *dolly*. No distinction has been made between tracking, traveling, and dollying. Finally, the *zoom-lens* is sometimes used to produce movement similar to a tracking shot. However, a zoom in place of a track will often be apparent because a zoom "track" will change the depth of field of the shot while the real track will keep the depth of field constant. (*Depth of field* is defined as the area from camera to object and beyond that is seen in focus.) In the shot analysis of "An Occurrence at Owl Creek Bridge," no distinction has been made between a track and a zoom "track."

CAMERA ANGLES

The camera can be set up prior to the shot or moved during the shot to obtain certain angles. The shot in which the camera is parallel to the subject is considered the norm and is not noted in the shot analysis. In a *low-angle* shot (LA), the camera is tilted upward on its axis; in a *high-angle shot* (HA), the camera is tilted downward. Since some shots are slightly angled or acutely angled, this may also be noted (SLA, AHA). In the shot analysis, camera angles have been placed in parentheses and follow the distance notation of the shot (84 LS (LA)).

SOUND

Although "The Bridge" was made in 1931–1932, the sound consists of nonsynchronous music only. On the other hand, "An Occurrence at Owl Creek Bridge" has dialogue, music, local sound, and sound effects, both synchronous and nonsynchronous. Particularly meaningful sound is noted in the shot analysis at the point at which it occurs.

As was noted at the beginning of this introduction, the shot analysis should not be thought of as a duplication of the experience of seeing the film. Many of the descriptions of the visuals and sounds are subjective and selective. Thus, it is conceivable that other shot analyses of these films would emphasize certain visual elements or describe certain sounds in different ways. Hopefully, however, distortions have been kept at a minimum.

GERALD R. BARRETT

THOMAS L. ERSKINE

Shot Analysis:
"The Bridge" ("The Spy")

1   Fade-in on credits.

> THE BRIDGE
> Based on a story by
> AMBROSE BIERCE
> Adapted and Directed by
> CHARLES VIDOR

Dissolve

2

> Players
> NICHOLAS BELA
> CHARLES DARVAS
> Photography
> WILLIAM J. WHEELER

Fade-out

3   Fade-in. LS (HA). A small bridge seen in the distance
from down river. The bridge spans the meandering river at
a narrow point, and both ends of the bridge are hidden by

87

a dense covering of trees. A heavily treed hill is seen in the far distance beyond the bridge. (Appropriate musical selections are played throughout film.)

Dissolve   (9

4   LS. A marching column of soldiers seen through trees. The column enters the frame from the left and moves off camera to the right. A man in a white shirt with his hands tied behind him is in the column.

Dissolve   (10

5   MS. Soldiers and man in white shirt walking toward and past camera.

Dissolve   (7

6   MCU. Tracking shot of civilian walking in the center of a cluster of soldiers. He appears ill-at-ease as he glances at the ground in front of him and then looks to the soldiers on his left and then on his right.

Dissolve   (10

7   LS. The column continues to march toward the camera, which is placed on one side of the road. The stone wall marking the entrance to the bridge is seen on the other side. Large trees with luxuriant foliage frame the scene.

(6

8   MLS. The column marches onto the bridge toward the camera with the commanding officer in the lead and a drummer directly behind him. The officer abruptly stops, wheels around, and faces the column. The soldiers stop, turn away from the wall of the bridge, and come to attention. They take one step back, leaving the civilian by himself and directly facing the officer.

(10

9   CU. The civilian looks to his right at the soldiers standing at attention and then looks at the officer.

(4

10 MLS. The drummer, the officer, and the civilian are positioned on a diagonal line in the left half of the frame. The officer quickly turns from the civilian and faces the drummer.

(5

11 CU. The tense civilian looks up into the trees and then at the officer.

(2

12 MLS. The officer turns from the drummer and walks past the civilian to the other side of the bridge.

(4

13 CU. The civilian nervously watches the officer's movements.

(2

14 MCU. With his back to the camera, the officer walks to the wall of the bridge and peers at the river below.

(4

15 CU. The civilian intently watches the officer.

(2

16 MS. The officer continues to look down at the river. He partly turns toward a soldier in the column and gives a command.

(4

17 LS. The civilian is in the center of the frame with the column lined up on a diagonal behind him. A soldier at the far end of the line walks across to the officer, and the civilian intensely watches.

(2

18 (=15)

(3

19 MS. The officer is in the right foreground with his back to the camera, and the soldier is facing him and carefully listening to his directions. A second soldier comes into the

frame, stands next to the first soldier, and takes the bayonet off his rifle. The first soldier begins to wedge the bayonet into a crack in the stone wall.

(6

20   CU (SHA). The civilian watches.

(4

21   CU. The bayonet is hammered into the crack with the rifle butt.

(3

22   (=20)

(5

23   MS. The soldiers complete their task.

(1

24   CU. The civilian looks on intently.

(2

25   MS. The first soldier stands between the officer and the second soldier. He takes a coil of rope off his shoulder and walks in the direction of the civilian.

(5

26   CU (SLA). The civilian watches the approaching soldier. His head is down, but he is looking up at the soldier. The other soldiers stand at attention behind the civilian. The soldier walks to his side and looks down at him. The civilian turns his head and looks up into the eyes of the soldier. The soldier places the noose around his neck, tightens it, and looks in the direction of his commanding officer. The panicked civilian looks pleadingly at the soldier and then, open-mouthed, in the direction of the officer.

(11

27   MS. The officer glares toward the civilian as the second soldier looks on. The officer moves his head slightly, signifying that the civilian should be taken to the wall.

(3

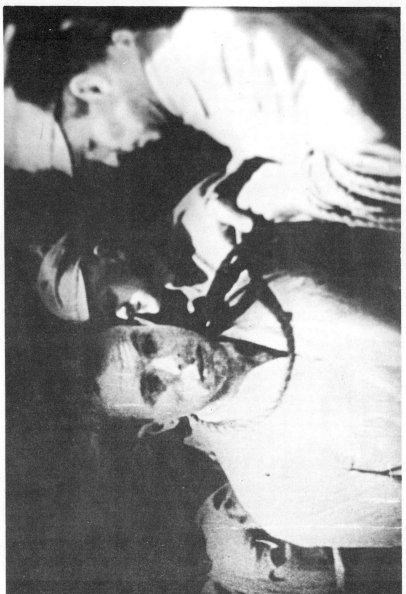

Shot 26

28   MS. The first soldier turns the civilian and leads him off
     camera towards the wall.

                                                                 (3

29   MLS. The end of the wall bathed in sunlight. The soldier
     leads the civilian into the frame and helps him to climb
     onto the wall.

                                                                 (10

30   MS. The officer walks off camera towards the column of
     soldiers.

                                                                 (4

31   MS. The wall forms a diagonal across the frame. The first
     soldier, holding coils of rope in his hand, walks along the
     chest-high wall. The body of the civilian is above the
     frame, but we see his feet walking along the top of the
     wall.

                                                                 (3

32   CU. The civilian looks down toward the water. The bot-
     tom of the frame cuts off his face below the eyes; the upper
     part of the frame is filled with trees overhead.

                                                                 (4

33   MS. The first soldier ties the rope to the bayonet, which
     is secured to the wall. The civilian's feet on the wall are
     near his head.

                                                                 (2

34   CU. The civilian continues to look downward, looks over-
     head, turns his head further up and toward the side, and
     closes his eyes. The rope around his neck seems empha-
     sized by his movements; the background is pure-white.

                                                                 (3

35   MLS. The officer stands at attention in the foreground, his
     back to the camera. On his left, the column of soldiers
     forms a straight line into the background. On his right,
     the first soldier has completed tying the rope to the bayo-
     net; the second soldier stands at attention facing him. The

first soldier crosses the bridge and comes to attention at the end of the column. The second soldier turns and comes to attention in front of the civilian as he stands on the wall, his back to the soldiers.

(4

36 MLS (LA). The civilian seen from below the bridge as he looks downward. His figure is in the center of the frame, and he is surrounded by trees overhead.

(3

37 MS. Front view of the officer as he stares in the direction of the civilian. The first three soldiers in the column are on his left.

(3

38 MS (LA). The back of the civilian seen from the bridge as he looks downward. His figure is on the right side of the frame, the rest of which is filled with blowing trees. The top of the frame cuts off most of his head.

(2

39 (=37) The officer turns toward the first soldier in the column, the young drummer, and the youth begins a drum roll.

(2

40 MCU. The civilian looks downward, grimaces, and closes his eyes. This image is superimposed over a CU of the beating drum. The superimposed drum is irised into the lower right portion of the frame as the civilian puffs his cheeks and turns his head to the right of the frame. An iris-wipe expands from the circumference of the drum resulting in the following image: the beating drum in the lower right-hand portion of the frame, a CU of a woman in the left portion of the frame, smiling and looking in the direction of the drum, and a CU of a boy in the right-hand portion of the frame, above the drum, looking in the direction of the woman. An image of the civilian (=start of the shot) is in the center of the frame, between the

woman and the boy and over the drum. His chin appears
to be resting on the drum. The woman and boy are superimposed over the civilian, and the drum is superimposed
over both. All three images are in motion during this shot.

(18

41 (=end of 37) The officer places his hand on the drummer's shoulder; the youth turns away from the camera,
but continues the drum roll; the officer grasps the drummer's shoulder.

(3

42 ECU. The civilian with head down and eyes closed. The
boy in shot 40 is superimposed in the lower right-hand
corner of the frame.

(7

43 LS. Low angle back shot of the civilian standing on the
wall. A soldier in the lower left-hand portion of the frame
is prodding him off the wall with his rifle.

(¾

44 MS (LA). The civilian dropping off the wall. The background is white.

(2

45 CU. The civilian falls downward in a blur: the midsection,
the chest, the head. The rope tightens and the face looks
upward. The twisting river is in the background.

(¾

46 ECU. Side view of the woman smiling at the boy.

(½—9 fr

47 ECU. Side view of the woman holding the boy in her
arms.

(½—9 fr

48 ECU. The boy screaming.

(½—9 fr

49   ECU. The head of the civilian twisting at the end of the
     rope.

                                                        (¾

50   ECU. The screaming boy being comforted by the woman's
     hand on his cheek.

                                                   (½ —8 fr

51   ECU. A rope, in the center of the frame, breaks. The lower
     half falls away, leaving a white frame.

                                                 (½ —10 fr

52   ECU. The head of the civilian, twisting at the end of the
     rope, suddenly falls out of the frame.

                                                        (½

53   MS. The body plunges into the water.

                                                        (2

54   CU. Turbulent water. The civilian surfaces in the lower
     part of the frame, gasping for breath. He looks toward the
     camera and appears frightened.

                                                        (5

55   CU. A soldier looking downward, preparing to fire his rifle.

                                                        (1

56   (=end of 54) The civilian takes a breath and plunges
     underwater.

                                                        (2

57   ECU (HA). Zip diagonal of water.

                                                        (3

58   CU (HA). The civilian surfaces, looking toward the
     camera.

                                                        (3

59   MCU (LA). Two soldiers viewed from the eyes up. Cloud
     of gunsmoke. Most of the frame is composed of trees and
     sky behind them.

                                                        (¾

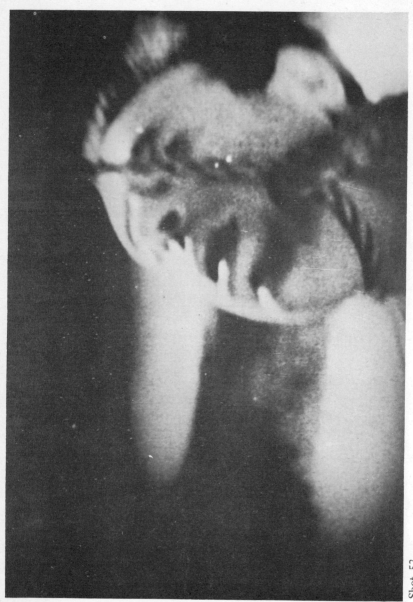

Shot 52

Permission by Raymond Rohauer

Shot 54

60   (=58) The civilian again plunges underwater.

(1

61   ECU (HA). Zip diagonal of water.

(5

62   CU. Reeds floating in water. The civilian's head rises out
     of the water among the reeds, and he looks around in the
     general direction of the camera. He plunges underwater
     again.

(15

63   MS (HA). A single reed in the water. It is suddenly thrust
     up at a right angle to the surface.

(5

64   MCU (LA). Three soldiers viewed from the eyes up.
     Most of the frame is composed of trees behind them.

(2

65   MCU. The reed moves against the current. The far bank
     of the river is in the background.

(4

66   (=64) A cloud of smoke from gunfire.

(¾

67   (=65) The reed suddenly goes underwater.

(1

68   MS (HA). Rippling water reflecting trees.

(9

69   LS (HA). A river bank. The land is covered with very tall
     grass and the civilian moves through the grass toward the
     camera. His hands are tied behind his back, and he
     attempts to free himself. He moves out of the right side
     of the frame.

(30

70   MS. The civilian moves into the frame from the left,
     kneels down with his back to the camera, and manages to
     free his hands by sawing the rope on a rock in the fore-

ground. He turns toward the camera and rests against the rock. Breathing heavily, he falls face downward and rests.

(33

71 CU. The civilian's head in profile, his lips touching the ground. He opens his eyes, stares at the ground, and lifts his head.

(20

72 MS (HA). Civilian lifting his head and looking around him. He rubs his wrists, turns his head toward the sky, closes his eyes, and looks down and around, shaking his head slightly.

(28

73 MS (HA). Civilian in profile. He is crouched at the bottom of the frame, surrounded by short grass and weeds. He gets to his feet and the camera tilts with him. He takes the remaining pieces of rope off his wrists, looks forward, and strides off camera right.

(9

74 LS. A path through a clearing of bushes and flowers in bloom. The civilian begins to pick some flowers.

(5

75 MS. The happy civilian looks down at a flowering bush and plucks the blooms. He gathers them in one hand, smiles down at them, and raises his arms in exuberance, lifting his head back and laughing. He looks down at the flowers again, smiles and strides past the camera.

(19

76 LS. A heavily shaded path. The civilian walks toward the camera as it tracks back. He smiles, plucking flowers as he goes. He jumps in the air, bends down, picks up a stick, and waves it overhead. He puts the stick over his shoulder and strides in an imitation of a soldier with a rifle. He waves the stick overhead again and pauses.

(32

77   MS. The civilian takes the stick off his shoulder and aims
     it as he would a rifle. He grasps the "barrel" with flowers
     still clutched in his hand. He pretends to shoot, laughs,
     spins around, and tosses the stick into the underbrush. He
     points to the flight of the stick, laughs, and salutes.

                                                                    (13

78   LS. The smiling civilian continues to stride along the path
     in the direction of the tracking camera. Suddenly he stops
     and wheels around.

                                                                     (3

79   MCU. The civilian, no longer smiling, glances back over
     his shoulder.

                                                                     (2

80   LS. The civilian continues to glance over his shoulder and
     runs off the path into the woods. The camera pans with
     him as he runs between the bushes and trees.

                                                                    (17

81   LS. A clearing in the woods. The panning camera follows
     the civilian as he runs through the clearing and into dense
     clusters of trees and bushes.

                                                                    (10

82   LS. A hilly terrain covered with bushes and trees. The
     camera pans and tilts as the civilian continues to run.

                                                                    (12

83   LS (LA). He jumps over a gully.

                                                                     (2

84   LS (LA). The camera tilts to follow him in profile down a
     steep hill. He slides to the bottom of the hill and lies there.

                                                                     (3

85   CU. The civilian lies face down on the side of a road. He
     lifts his head and faces the camera. He breathes heavily,
     looks ahead of him, and quickly rises.

                                                                     (2

86   LS. He quickly gets up and runs past the camera.

                                                                     (1

Shot 80

87   LS (LA). He runs down the road past the camera.

(4

88   MS. The camera tracks in front of him as he runs down the road with his hand outstretched. His breathing is labored and he staggers slightly, but he continues to run.

(9

89   LS. The camera tracks down the empty road in front of him. LS superimposition of the woman and boy (40) smiling and running in a circle. This superimposition dissolves into a LS superimposition of the woman and boy sitting and talking.

(8

90   MS. The civilian continues to run down the road as the camera tracks in front of him.

(4

91   LS. The camera tracks down the empty road in front of him. LS superimposition of the woman holding the boy in her arms. They are in a field and semireclined. Superimposition fades out, leaving track of empty road.

(1

92   (=90)

(6

93   LS. The camera tracks down the empty road in front of him. LS superimposition of the woman who is seated with the boy in her arms and is rocking him slightly.

(3

94   (=90) The civilian stretches his hand out, and his running seems labored.

(2

95   CU. Heads of woman and child superimposed over tracking shot of empty road. Superimposition fades out, leaving track of empty road.

(2

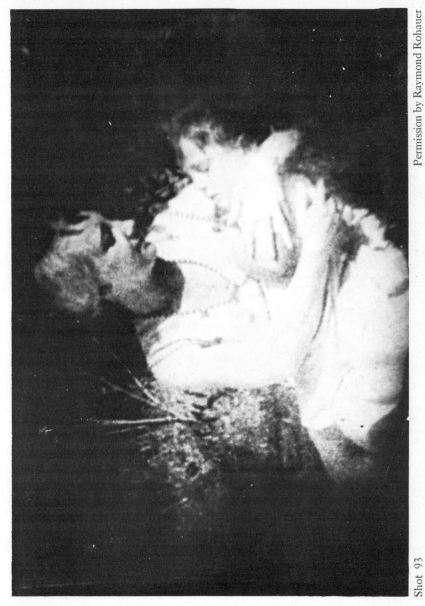

Shot 93

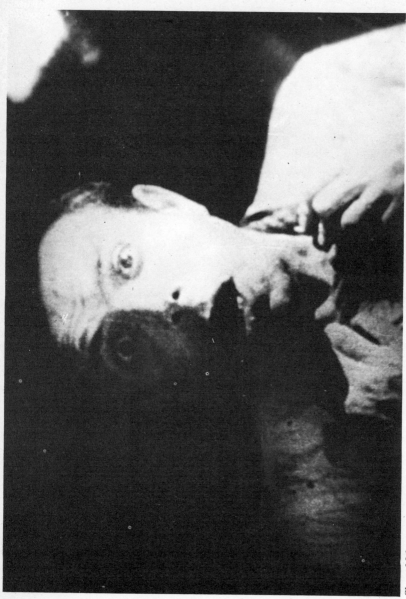

Shot 106

96 (=90) The civilian begins to stagger, and he thrashes about as he runs.

(3

97 LS. Woman with child walking superimposed over a shot of a grassy clearing backed by trees.

(1

98 LS (LA). The civilian, arms outstretched and smiling, looks off the road into the trees.

(1

99 (=97) The woman and child begin to move off camera.

(1

100 (=98) The civilian gestures imploringly.

(¾

101 LS. Woman and child walking away, superimposed over the road.

(½

102 MS. The civilian, arms outstretched, hands open, looks stunned.

(¾

103 (=101) The woman and child are farther down the road.

(¾

104 CU. The civilian looking toward the camera with a pained expression. The background is black.

(¾

105 LS. The road is now empty.

(¾

106 CU. The civilian looks puzzled. His features tighten as a superimposed beating drum fades in. He looks up, shocked, stretches his neck, and pulls on the rope around his neck. His eyes bulge and his mouth twists and opens wide.

(7

107 CU. Superimpositions of the beating drum and the woman holding the child over an image of a cloudy sky. The woman/child shot = 47.

(½ —9 fr

108 CU. Superimposition of the beating drum over the shot of the woman and child = 46.

(½ —9 fr

109 CU. Superimposition of the beating drum over the shot of the screaming child = 48.

(½ —8 fr

110 CU. Superimposition of the beating drum over image of the head of the hanging civilian. The head continues to twist and the drum continues to beat.

(4

111 MS. The drummer, facing the camera in frame left, finishes his drum roll. The officer is in the center of the frame with his back to the camera. The drummer boy turns to attention at the head of the column of soldiers. The column turns to attention, their backs to the camera. Half of the column steps over to form a second column in front of the officer. The soldiers march away from the camera and off the bridge.

(7

112 CU. Attached to the bayonet, sticking in the stone wall, is a paper blowing in the breeze. On the paper is one word: SPY!

(2

113 LS. The body of the civilian is seen hanging from the bridge. The body sways slightly.

Fade-out (4

114 Fade-in.   FINIS

GERALD R. BARRETT
THOMAS L. ERSKINE

Shot Analysis:
"An Occurrence at Owl Creek Bridge"

1   (Drum roll.) Fade-in. CU. A burnt tree trunk with the
    following credits superimposed:

> A Cappagariff Release
> Marcell Ichac
> and
> Paul de Roubaix
> present

Credits fade out and camera tilts up the trunk to a sign.
(End drum roll.)

> ORDER
> ANY CIVILIAN
> CAUGHT INTERFERING WITH
> THE RAILROAD BRIDGES
> TUNNELS OR TRAINS WILL BE
> SUMMARILY HANGED
> The 4th of April, 1862

(Drum roll.) Diagonal up trunk to the jagged end where
it has been broken off. Bare stumpy branches from another
tree in left foreground, darkened woods and sky in the
distance. The following superimposed credits fade in.
(End drum roll.)

AN OCCURRENCE
AT
OWL CREEK BRIDGE
A Film by Robert Enrico

Credits fade out.

(36

2   ELS (LA). Bare tree branches against a glary sky.
     (Screeches of owls in the distance throughout the shot.)
     Diagonal downward past tree trunk to more trees on the
     side of a hill set against the sky. Ground-level lateral track
     right through the mist past trees. A bridge is seen below
     in the distance. (Trumpet plays reveille. Military com-
     mands.)

(40

3   ELS. Lateral track right past more trees in the mist. The
     bridge is in the distance. (Military commands, sound of
     footsteps on bridge. Screeches of owls. The sounds of
     activity and of nature are unnaturally loud throughout the
     film.) Trees and branches are passed in the foreground.

(19

4   ELS (LA). Lateral track right past a sentinel standing
     on large boulder in the distance. Trees and branches are
     passed in the foreground.

(12

5   ELS. Lateral track right through trees to a HA view of
     soldiers marching away from the camera onto a wooden
     bridge spanning a deep river. They continue over the
     bridge and stand in file on the far river bank to the left
     of the bridge. Their camp, one large white tent, is seen
     in the right background.

(36

6   MCU. Profile of a lieutenant standing at the head of the
     file and looking towards the bridge. The sentinel is stand-
     ing on a high ridge in the distance, silhouetted against the

Shot 5

Shot 8

sky, looking down at the river. A slight lateral track left and slow pan right discloses the file of soldiers standing at attention and facing the bridge. (Screeches of owls.)

(9

7   MS. Profile of soldier walking, rope in hand, past lieuten- ant toward the bridge. Camera pans with him and then tracks from behind and passes a guard standing at attention and facing away from the bridge. The soldier walks onto the bridge (screeches of owls) as the track stops. Another soldier is marching onto the bridge from the far side. There is a plank at the center of the bridge, placed across the rails.

(14

8   ELS (HA). Side view of the bridge. A bound civilian is being escorted onto the bridge by two soldiers, one on his right and one behind him. (Screeches of owls.) They move to the center of the bridge and face the near railing. The sergeant awaits them.

(15

9   CU. The bound man, looking downward towards the river, slowly raises his head, stares into space, and looks overhead.

(7

10 MS (LA). A rope is thrown over one of the timbers of the trestle overhead. (Very loud sound made by the rope as it is thrown over the trestle.) Diagonal down to MS (HA) of a soldier putting the end of the rope through a slip knot and pulling it tight to the timber above. During the diagonal we see the file of soldiers standing on the bank at parade rest and a captain overseeing the action on the bridge.

(16

11 MCU (ALA). The soldier is shaping the noose. He is framed by the timbers of the trestle seen against a glary white sky, and we see his face through the noose.

(8

Shot 11

Shot 12

12   MLS (SHA). The captain, with his back to us in the center of the frame, the plank jutting off the bridge to his right, and the civilian, with a soldier on either side, in profile. The sergeant is standing on the plank at the railing, continuing to prepare the rope. The captain walks past the civilian, stands on the plank, turns around and faces its far end. The two soldiers lead the man over the railing onto the plank and turn him around so that he faces the captain.

(19

13   MCU. The hands of one soldier untie the man's cravat, remove it, and flatten his shirt collar. The hands of another soldier loop the noose over the man's neck and tighten it. The man looks toward the soldier and then looks down.

(20

14   MCU (AHA). Front view of lower legs and feet standing on the end of the plank over the river below. The feet are facing the bridge and are placed at a 45 degree angle within the frame. The camera turns around the legs and feet in a quarter circle and pans away from the plank to a AHA view of the water below.

(8

15   ECU. The lieutenant at the head of the file flexes his hands as they rest on his sword. (Loud sounds of birds.)

(4

16   CU (SLA). The captain looks up toward the rope on the trestle.

(8

17   MCU. The civilian looks to his left toward the file of soldiers on the river bank. The steep side of the ravine is seen behind him, a crescent of sky is overhead. He blinks and stares.

(7

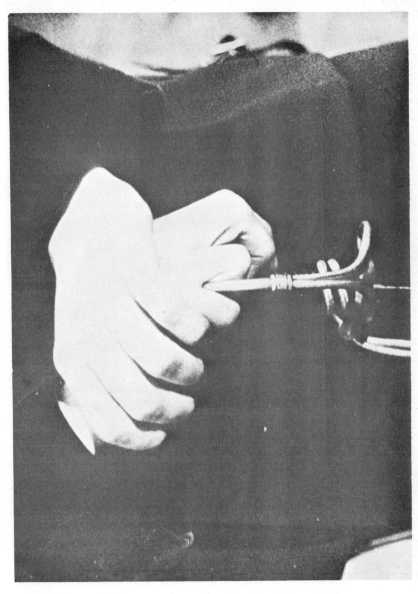

18 LS. From the bridge. The file of soldiers is seen through the timbers of the trestle. Camera pans right and tracks forward past the timbers in the foreground and the file in the distance to the soldier at attention, his back to the bridge. He faces the white tent directly in front of him and his form is silhouetted against it.

(15

19 CU. The man continues to stare and then turns his head to observe the guard on the other end of the bridge.

(4

20 LS. From the bridge. Slow track towards the guard as he faces at attention, his back to the bridge.

(5

21 CU. The man continues to stare, then quickly turns his head slightly behind him and to his left. Zip diagonal up to the sentinel standing on the hill in the distance seen against the bare branches of small trees, silhouetted against the sky.

(7

22 MCU. The civilian's legs are being bound together above the knees by a strip of cloth. Tilt down past the bridge railing to CU (SHA) of a stooping soldier tying the civilian's ankles together with a similar cloth strip. The river below is seen in the background.

(9

23 LS (HA). The civilian on the plank seen from a position on the hill behind and to the right of the file. The bridge in the distance is in the upper left portion of the frame; the lower half of the entire frame is filled by a cannon set at an angle so that the muzzle is directly under the figure of the civilian. Lateral track past the cannon toward the bridge and tilt down to a LS (HA) of the file with the bridge in the distance.

(22

24 (=end of 22) The soldier finishes tying the civilian's ankles and moves back out of the frame. The top of the frame is cut off by the railing of the bridge, the civilian's feet shuffle on the plank as it springs slightly. The river below reflects trees.

(8

25 LS (HA). A piece of driftwood floating downstream.

(6

26 CU. The civilian, head turned to his left, watches the floating driftwood, turns his face forward, grimaces, and closes his eyes.

(6

27 LS. The hills in the distance meet in a "V" in the center of the frame. The sun glares at the meeting point. (Loud sounds of birds.)

(4

28 MCU. (Loud sounds of birds.) The captain looks over his shoulder into the woods and then turns his head forward to face the civilian.

(6

29 MLS (AHA). The action at the center of the bridge. The captain faces the civilian as both stand in profile on the plank. Two soldiers stand at the captain's right in the foreground, facing him. A third soldier on the other side of the plank in the background does likewise. The captain is the center of attention. The soldier in the background moves foreward, clicks his heels, stands up on the plank, turns, and faces the civilian. The captain moves off the plank and takes the soldier's position.

(15

30 CU (SHA). Profile shot of the soldier's feet on one end of the plank. Pan right to the civilian's feet on the other end. Tilt up body coupled with slow zoom ending in a

tight three-quarter CU of the civilian with his eyes closed. (We hear a woman's name spoken softly.)

(28

31 MLS. In the left foreground the civilian's wife is sitting in a rocking chair and doing needlework. (We hear her name twice again, but spoken much more loudly than in shot 30. A metronome-like sound increases in speed and volume throughout the shot.) A boy is pushing a girl on a swing in the right middleground. A large house fills the background of the frame. All appear to be calm and contented, and the light and full foliage indicate a soft spring day. The camera tracks laterally so that the woman is centered. As it begins to move, the woman looks up, smiles, moves out of her chair, and happily advances (needlework in hand), toward the camera. She is wearing an elaborate spring dress with a long shawl draped over her shoulders. The children continue to play on the swing behind her as she moves toward the camera to a MCU. All of this is in slow motion.

(27

32 MCU. (Off camera: the captain tells one of his soldiers to take the civilian's watch.) The civilian, heavy rope around his neck, gasps and hands arrange the knot to the back of his neck. He looks down.

(5

33 CU. A soldier's hand reaches into a pocket of his brocade vest and pulls out an encased watch. It is opened, disclosing the face, and the watch plays a tune. The camera pans as the case is snapped shut and passed to the right. The hands of a second soldier are seen as he takes the watch, places it in a leather case attached to his belt, and pats the case. (The soldiers are commanded to come to attention.)

(15

34 ELS (HA). The bridge through the trees from a position on the bank opposite the file of soldiers.

(10

Shot 31

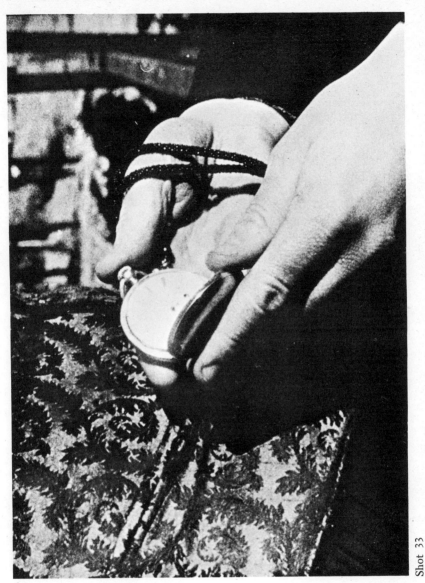

35   LS (LA). The figures on the bridge from the bank on the file's side of the river. The underside of the bridge is seen in the bottom half of the frame.

(8

36   ECU (SLA). The civilian's face, eyes open and lips quivering.

(18

37   ECU. The civilian's bound hands behind his back (out of view of the soldiers on the bridge), twisting and pulling at the ropes. (Sound of his gasps off camera.)

(7

38   MS. The captain, facing the camera, looks in the civilian's direction, turns his head in the direction of the soldier on the other end of the plank, and quickly but firmly nods his head.

(4

39   CU. The soldier's feet on the plank fill the right side of the frame. The plank is set at a diagonal, and we see the civilian's legs on the other end in the upper left of the frame. The soldier's heels click, turn, and step off the plank and out of frame right. The plank springs up and the body of the civilian drops down out of frame left.

(5

40   LS (LA). The bridge seen from the river. The body continues its descent.

(1

41   CU (AHA). Zooming shot of the civilian's legs as he nears and hits the water. (Gong-like sound.)

(2

42   MLS (LA). Underwater view of the body as it hits the water and plunges down past the camera. It tilts down as the body plunges deeper. (Exaggerated sound of bubbles, which continues through shot 55.)

(4

Shot 40

Shot 41

43. MCU. The civilian drops down through the frame. The frayed rope from the noose dangles overhead. The camera tilts with him as he continues to drop.

(4

44 LS (LA). Turbulence created by the falling body, the light reflecting off the surface overhead. The body continues to plunge.

(5

45 MS. The body in a horizontal position begins to pass the camera. The frayed rope dangles in the foreground. The camera tilts down with the falling body and moves into a MCU of the civilian holding his breath and looking upward. The camera stops and the body continues to fall deeper.

(8

46 LS (LA). View of the glare of sunlight on the surface of the water directly overhead. Tilt down to falling body.

(8

47 CU. The body is in a horizontal position with the top of the head in the foreground. The civilian struggles into an upright position and works the ropes off his hands. With air bubbles trailing upward, he unloosens the noose from around his neck, thrusts it off his head, and begins to swim toward the surface. As the top of his body moves past the top of the frame, he begins to kick with his bound legs.

(22

48 LS. Side view of the civilian struggling toward the surface through a watery shaft of light.

(4

49 CU. The civilian, straining to hold his breath and looking upward through the air bubbles, reaches down to untie his bound legs. The camera tilts down to his legs as he struggles to free himself.

(8

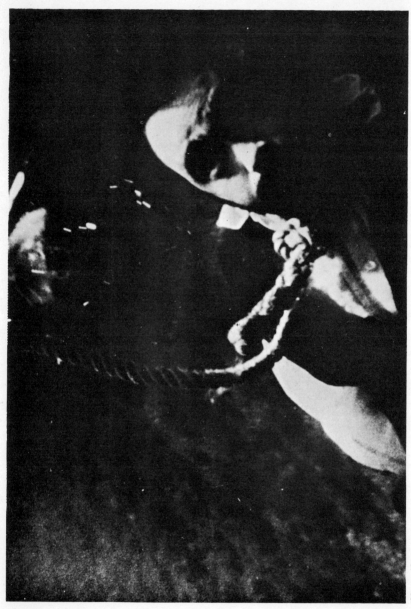

Shot 43

50 MCU. Profile of the civilian's face as he holds his breath and fights to free his legs. His head is in a horizontal position in the frame and he turns it from side to side as he grimaces.

(4

51 CU. He loosens the bonds from around his legs and kicks them off as the camera tilts upward with the action.

(7

52 MCU. The civilian's head and shoulders are horizontal in the frame as he twists, turns, and stretches in an effort to take his boots off while continuing to hold his breath.

(3

53 MCU. Tugging at his boots with both hands. Finally, the boots slip off and the camera tilts down to follow them as they drop down towards the bottom.

(16

54 MLS. The camera tilts upward as the civilian swims to the surface of the water at the top of the frame and breaks the sunlit surface.

(7

55 MCU. View from above the water. The civilian breaks the surface of the water with head thrown back, shrieks for air, and bobs and sputters. He then shakes his head and looks upward and around him. His gaze rests upward in the direction of the river bank off to the left. (Off camera: A man, accompanied by a guitar, sings a folk song about what it means to be alive and to respond to nature. The song continues to shot 62.)

(27

56 MCU. A tree branch covered with leaves. Out-of-focus leafy branches in the background. Camera pans right past more leafy branches in the foreground, gently blowing in the breeze.

(6

57 CU. Camera pans right and zooms in on one leaf on a branch dramatically lit by the sunlight.

(5

58 ECU. One leaf, made translucent by the sunlight behind it, fills the frame. A thousand-legger slowly crawls over its surface.

(5

59 ECU. A blade of grass with jewel-like drops of dew on it is in the foreground. The blurred background is brought into focus, disclosing a broad leaf covered with sparkling drops of dew.

(7

60 ECU. More sparkling vegetation. Camera zooms in from out of focus to in focus to out of focus.

(8

61 CU. A spider weaving a web. The web and spider are dramatically lit.

(7

62 ECU. The weaving, semi-translucent spider fills the frame. (Sound of owl.)

(7

63 LS (LA). The bridge as seen from the bank. It is silhouetted against the glary sky. A soldier moves onto the bridge in slow motion. The camera pans left with him as he nears the center of the bridge, leans over the railing and looks down towards the water. The camera continues to pan toward the trestled center of the bridge to view the other soldiers rushing about in slow motion. (Garbled commands.)

(19

64 LS (LA). The file facing towards the river. The lieutenant holds his sword before him at attention, and the soldiers load their rifles in a faster slow motion. Other soldiers rush about behind them. (More commands, less garbled and more natural.)

(13

Shot 61

Shot 63

65   LS (LA). The captain in the center of the bridge pointing toward the camera (in the direction of the civilian). As the camera zooms out, the other soldiers on the bridge run to the captain, stand next to him, and aim guns toward the camera. The motion is faster than in the previous shot, but still slow. (Commands continue.)

(13

66   MCU. Quick zoom to CU of civilian's face, looking up toward the bridge. (Off camera: The captain calls the civilian by his name, Peyton Farquhar, and tells him there is no hope for escape. The captain's words echo in Farquhar's mind during the next shot.)

(4

67   LS (LA). Three soldiers are on the bridge: one has a rifle and is in the center of frame; another, the captain, looks straight ahead; as the camera zooms in to focus on the soldier with the rifle, the third soldier passes from left to right behind him. The soldier with the rifle aims his gun.

(4

68   MCU. The civilian, treading water, continues to stare at the action on the bridge.

(4

69   CU. The soldier, taking slow and careful aim, pulls back the hammer of his gun.

(4

70   (=66)

(4

71   ECU. The civilian's eye.

(3

72   MS. The soldier aims his rifle, fires, is almost obscured by a cloud of smoke, lowers his rifle, and looks in the direction of the civilian.

(1

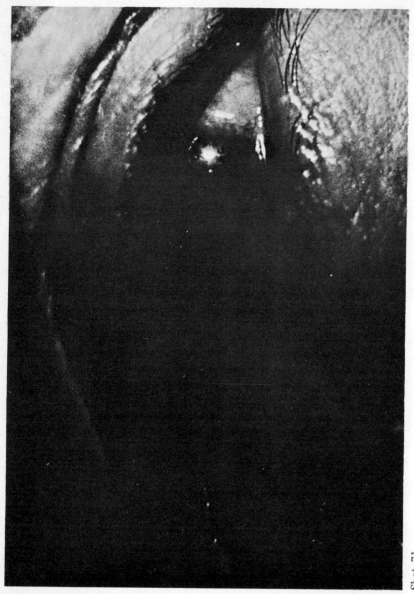

Shot 71

73 MS (HA). Farquhar swimming away from camera, which follows his progress.

(7

74 MCU. Another soldier moves into frame, aims his pistol, shoots, and moves to his left as camera pans with him. Standing between two bridge supports, he quickly aims his pistol and fires.

(5

75 LS. As Farquhar swims upstream against the current and toward the camera, it diagonals through a cloud of smoke and up a hill to the soldiers at the top of the hill. Camera tracks laterally left past trees between the river and the file.

(9

76 CU. The lieutenant at the head of the file with his sword held upright; his right hand grasps its hilt and he shouts a command.

(2

77 MCU. A side view of the lieutenant watching Farquhar. Suddenly, he points his sword forward in a command to fire.

(3

78 MS (LA). Side view of rifle barrels in file pointed at the river. The rifles sweep downward to the right, taking aim at Farquhar.

(3

79 CU. The lieutenant commands his troops to fire.

(2

80 LS (LA). File seen from Farquhar's position through the trees. Camera tracks laterally left as they fire.

(2

81 LS (LA). Farquhar seen from behind through tree trunks (file's view) as the camera tracks laterally along the bank. The smoke from the rifle fire drifts through the trees.

The camera continues to track behind him as he swims quickly away and dives under water.

(14

82   LS. Farquhar seen underwater swimming under a submerged tree trunk and moving toward the camera. He swims up again to the surface.

(2

83   MS. Farquhar, seen from behind, breaks above the water and frantically continues to swim away from the camera.

(7

84   LS (LA). View from the river through the trees as the camera quickly tracks laterally with the cannoneer as he follows Farquhar's progress.

(6

85   MS. Pan with Farquhar seen from the side as he swims on a horizontal line across the frame, right to left.

(7

86   LS (LA). View from the river through the trees as the camera quickly tracks laterally past the cannoneer, who fires.

(4

87   LS (HA). The river in Farquhar's area as the missile shatters the water.

(2

88   CU (HA). The splattered water fills the frame. The camera tilts up to a MS of Farquhar seen as he swims away from the turbulent water. He stops swimming, raises his arm in the air, and sinks under the surface. He immediately comes up for air and sluggishly continues to swim. Suddenly, he pauses and looks in front of him.

(7

89   MS (HA). A water snake coiling through the water towards Farquhar.

(4

90   LS. The camera is placed on the surface of the water and Farquhar dives under the surface. Tilt down underwater to MS of Farquhar swimming toward and past the camera.

(4

91   LS (HA). Farquhar swimming away from camera underwater as seen from above the surface. Camera tilts up to follow.

(7

92   LS (LA). Profile shot of sentry perched atop the rock following Farquhar's progress. He aims his rifle and fires.

(2

93   MS (SHA). Farquhar thrashing through the water away from camera. (Sound of gunfire.) His progress is followed by a zoom-in as he starts to swim in a circle and ends in a CU swimming towards the camera as it zooms out.

(27

94   LS (ALA). Trees and sky spinning overhead. The shot ends on the blank and glary sky.

(12

95   LS. Farquhar in the swiftly running current. Camera pans right and we see him from behind as he tumbles along the surface in the distance.

(10

96   LS (HA). Side view of Farquhar in the boiling rapids. The camera pans right with him as he is rolled over submerged boulders and thrashes off. His figure is insignificant in the center of the frame.

(7

97   LS (HA). Front view of Farquhar as seen from the rocky bank. He slides over a submerged rock shelf, and the camera pans with him as he drops over a foaming fall and is lost in the white water directly in front of the camera. The camera remains static but no figure appears on the

surface. Fast pan downriver. Farquhar comes up in calmer water and is carried further downstream.

(20

98 LS (HA). Camera pans right following Farquhar thrashing through the foaming current.

(5

99 LS (HA). Farquhar is seen from behind in somewhat calmer water. Camera diagonals with him as he wearily swims towards land in the distance.

(18

100 MS. Camera tracks right along the hilly bank until Farquhar is disclosed in LS in a peaceful inlet. Track continues as he drags himself to the beach. The camera remains static as he pulls himself half out of the water and, after a few feeble and futile attempts to move himself, gives up.

(35

101 MCU. Farquhar lying on the beach; the top of his head is closest to the camera; his hand, clenching sand, extends into the foreground. He begins to lift his head.

(11

102 CU. Similar view of Farquhar. He looks down in front of him in the direction of his clenched fist and begins to laugh.

(9

103 ECU. Farquhar's hand open on the sand; the back of his hand is cut. His fingers score the sand as he clenches them into a fist. He spreads his fingers again and touches the ground with his palm and digs into the sand.

(12

104 MS (SHA). Farquhar's back fills the lower half of the frame, while the river bank is seen in the top half. His arms are spread above his head and he begins to clutch handfuls of sand and joyfully toss them overhead.

(13

Shot 101

105 LS. Three-quarter front view of Farquhar happily pounding the ground and thrashing his feet. He begins to crawl up the beach towards the camera. When he is in the center of the frame, he wildly and ecstatically rolls over and over in the sand. He ends up happily exhausted on his back in a spread-eagle position.

(30

106 MS (AHA). Farquhar's upper torso and face as seen from directly overhead. He looks up into the sky and laughs. (The "alive" theme [shot 55] is played on the guitar and continues through shot 108.)

(11

107 LS. Slowly spinning pan of the trees above, covered with leaves, softly moving in the breeze.

(12

108 LS (SHA). Farquhar lying on his back with his head in the direction of the camera. He rolls over on his elbows and crawls toward a flowered bush in the foreground as the camera tilts down to follow him. He carefully crawls up to the flower (MS), tilts it down toward his face, looks at it and smells it.

(36

109 ELS (AHA). The civilian is seen on the bank across the river in the upper portion of the frame. A shell explodes nearby and he runs into the trees that surround the bank.

(13

110 MS (ALA). The camera is placed at ground level and Farquhar runs into the frame from the top left and jumps over and past the camera. (A polyrhythmic, up-tempo, jazz-tinged drumming begins in this shot and continues through shot 114, where it is ended by the sound of an exploding missile.)

(2

111 LS. Against a background of woods Farquhar runs toward the camera, which slowly pans with him to the right. As he runs he looks from left to right. At a MS, he turns abruptly to the right, plunges into a thickly wooded area and the camera pans with him. He stumbles, falls, staggers to his feet, and resumes running. As he runs he is often partially obscured by out-of-focus trees and brush.*

(12

112 MCU. Farquhar continues to run to the right as the camera pans with him. The bushes and tree limbs through which he is seen are blurred, and he is periodically almost hidden behind them.

(11

113 LS. Farquhar still running to the right, emerges from the blurred background of trees, and as he runs the camera tracks laterally with him. He is again obscured by the trees.

(12

114 MS. Farquhar runs in a cleared area with the woods in the background. The camera tracks laterally with him as he continues running, now in cleared ground, now in underbrush. He veers toward the camera, stumbles, and falls behind a bush. The camera continues its track and diagonals down to the bush, seen out of focus.

(29

115 LS. A heavily wooded and shaded area. The camera tracks laterally left, and gradually Farquhar, once again running, is seen. Zoom in to MS of Farquhar, who has stopped running and is now supporting himself against a tree. He is gasping for breath and looks around behind him, as if expecting to see his pursuers. He then starts to run to his right, and the camera tracks with him as he runs through the wooded area in the background.

(14

* For a technical description of how some of the shots of Farquhar running through the woods were achieved, see *Screen Education Yearbook*, 1968, pp. 79–94.

Shot 112

116 LS. Farquhar runs to the left through a shaded, wooded area. (The drumming begins again and continues through shot 119.) The camera tracks laterally with him, then by him; and he veers left to a MS.

(14

117 MS. The camera pans with Farquhar in profile as he runs to the left. During the shot the shade makes Farquhar appear to be a running shadow.

(5

118 LS. Farquhar runs to the left behind trees in the foreground. As the camera pans left past a tree in the foreground, Farquhar moves toward the camera from the right of the frame, and it pans right with him as he passes in MS.

(3

119 LS. Woods with a tree trunk in the foreground center. Camera pans right as Farquhar runs past the tree trunk. He continues to run at full speed and to the right of the camera as it tracks backward with him. The camera stops as he staggers past in MS and pans right with him as he staggers and stumbles.

(19

120 MCU. A tree trunk fills three-quarters of the screen. Farquhar lurches into the frame from the left and falls against the trunk. Only his hands and the top of his head are seen. The camera pans left and tracks backward to a MS (HA) of the exhausted man kneeling with his arms around the tree. He pauses, takes a breath, gets to his feet, and staggers off frame right.

(14

121 LS. A fern-covered glen. Farquhar runs into the frame from the top left and bursts through the ferns. He passes the camera as it pans right with him, and he continues to run through the woods.

(5

122 ELS (SLA). A view of a straight road leading into the distance. The road, in shadow, is wooded on both sides by very tall straight trees, geometrically spaced, that fill the entire frame. There is a very limited view of the sky at the far end of the road (in the lower center of the frame). The effect is that of a series of cathedral-like arches, ending in an arched doorway of light. Farquhar's miniscule figure enters the arch, running at full speed, framed by the lighted doorway and the arched trees, and runs toward the camera. (The drumming begins again and becomes progressively louder as Farquhar nears the camera.) The camera tilts down as he gets closer and begins to track backward when he reaches a MS position. He struggles forward, running, staggering, gasping for breath, to a tight MS (LA) view. At that point he staggers and falls forward below the frame. (Drumming ends.) Camera tilts down to view his sprawled body, but the track continues at a uniform speed and stops about ten yards further down the road. Farquhar pushes himself to his feet and stumbles forward. (Sound of owls.)

(58

123 CU (HA). The camera tracks backward on a view of Farquhar's bare feet as he walks down the road.

(11

124 MCU (LA). Craning and rubbing his neck, Farquhar slowly and haltingly walks down the road towards the camera as it tracks back. The straight trees are overhead and behind him.

(19

125 LS. Track forward down the road; perfectly spaced trees on either side. A black square is at the apex of the road in the distance.

(6

126 MLS (LA). Farquhar walks, staggers, weaves down the road towards the camera which tracks back with him.

(14

Shot 122

127 CU (HA). Farquhar's plodding feet.

(12

128 MCU. Farquhar in semidarkness. As he walks ahead, the camera tracks back. He steps into the sunlight, stops, opens his eyes, looks intently in front of him, smiles, and walks ahead and past the camera.

(17

129 LS (LA). Farquhar, back to camera, walks forward as tall iron gates [pulled by ropes] open before him. He continues walking, breaks into a run, and moves off into the shadows up the road.

(12

130 MLS. Farquhar staggers through sunlit woods towards the camera.

(15

131 LS. The camera tracks through the branches of willow trees, brushing them as it passes, until the final branches are passed, allowing a view of the house (shot 31; another angle). (The "alive" theme resumes at a faster tempo and concludes at the end of the shot.) The camera tracks forward toward wife as she slowly comes off the porch and glides across a terrace towards it.

(22

132 MS. Farquhar sees her and runs forward while the camera slowly zooms back.

(5

133 LS. Three stone steps on the lawn at the side of the house. The camera is placed on the lower level. Track forward moving left as wife slowly moves into the frame from the right. The camera stops at the foot of the steps and wife slowly comes down the steps (MS) and begins to hold her hand out. She has a smile of anticipation on her face and is wearing the hooped and flowered dress as previously seen in shot 31. She looks off camera in Far-

Shot 129

quhar's direction. (A new musical motif, played on solo guitar, begins in this shot; the motif is joyful, but repetitive and insistent; it continues to the beginning of shot 140.)

(10

134 MS (LA). A long lens view of Farquhar running toward the camera. His figure fills about one-third of the frame. A leafy branch between Farquhar and the camera is seen out of focus. He is surrounded by darkness. As he moves forward, the camera zooms back but he moves faster than the zoom. He holds both hands out in an imploring gesture and his figure now fills about two-thirds of the frame.

(6

135 Basically the same shot as 132. However, it begins with wife already in the frame at the top of the steps. The end of the shot extends her action so that the MS is tighter. Further, her hand is more actively turned outward in a welcoming gesture. Her smile is rather enigmatic.

(9

136 Basically the same shot as 133. However, this shot is also carried further. It ends in a more angular MCU and Farquar moves his arms forward in a more frantically active gesture. Further, while he looked imploringly in 133, he looks deliriously happy here.

(6

137 This shot picks up the action of 132 and 134 as wife moves down the steps. However, it extends past the end of either shot, and the MS has become a MCU so that we do not see her hands. She tilts her head slightly to the side, and a look of recognition is seen on her face as she begins to walk forward and smile more broadly than in the previous shots.

(9

138 Basically the same shot as 135. However, the shot begins later and ends sooner. (In shots 132 to 137 there is a rhythmic contrast in movements within the frame. While

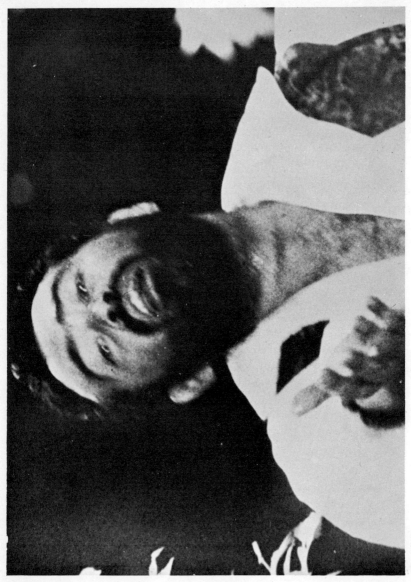

Shot 134

wife's movement seems constant from shot to shot,
Farquhar's seems to gradually speed up from shot to shot.)

(6

139 MCU. Three-quarter view of wife. Begins with wife at
the top of the stairs and she moves downward to the right.
The depth of field isolates her from the out-of-focus foliage
in the background. Pan right and track with her as she
moves in Farquhar's direction. She stops and leans her
head slightly forward. She smiles broadly in anticipation,
a tear glistening her cheek (CU, three-quarter view).

(20

140 MLS. Farquhar runs into the frame from the right and
calls his wife by name. He is in three-quarter view and
the camera tracks back in front of him towards wife. As
he reaches her (MS), the camera stops its track and we
view the rest of the shot from across wife's right shoulder.
Farquhar is in three-quarter view on the right, facing
towards the camera. Wife is in three-quarter view on the
left, facing away from the camera. They gaze lovingly at
one another and the music stops; he holds her arms at the
elbows, she moves her hands up his chest. She extends her
fingers, cupping them slightly and touches Farquhar at the
base of his neck. (A droning sound.) As she does so, he
jerks his head violently back, shouts, and continues to
fall down and back out of the frame. Wife holds her arms
up, fingers spread.

(11

141 MLS (SLA). Farquhar is in the center of the frame
backed by webs of bare branches. He is bound and bounces
up and down as the weight of his body pulls downward
against the rope around his broken neck. Zoom back to LS
(LA) of the body hanging from the bridge. The four
soldiers are standing and watching on the bridge above.
They come to attention at command, turn, and march off
left. The camera pans right to the bare trees on the bank.
The following fades in to create a superimposition.

Shot 140

ORDRE
TOUT CIVIL
supris a proximite des ponts,
tunnels ou voies ferrees
SERA PENDU
SANS JUGEMENT
Le 4 Avril 1862

The camera continues to pan right and the superimposition
fades out, followed by a fade-in of another superimposition:

LA RIVIERE du HIBOU
d' après
"An occurrence at
OWL CREEK bridge"
d'Ambrose Bierce
avec
Roger JACQUET

                                        Dissolve   (50

142 The camera continues to pan right and the superimposi-
    tion fades out, followed by a fade-in of another super-
    imposition:

Anne Cornally
Anker Larsen
Stephane Fey
Jean-Francois Zeller
Pierre Danny
Louis Adelin

Same direction as above:

Adaptations et
Mise en scene
de
Robert ENRICO

Same direction as above:

Images
de
Jean Bobbety

                                 Quick   Dissolve   (19

Shot 141

143 Lateral track right of more trees. The following superimposition fades in:

> Musique de
> Henri Lanoe
> avec
> Kenny Klarke
> Jimmy Gourley
> Cley Douglas
> Jean-Marie Imgrand
> Robert Escuras

Lateral track right continues and the superimposition
fades out followed by a fade-in of another superimposition:

Montage	Denise de Casabianca
	Robert Enrico
Mixage	Jean Neny
Assistant Realisateur	Nat Lilenstein
Assistant Operateur	Christian Guillouet
Regie	Pierre Lobreau
	Gerard Berger

Quick Dissolve   (18

144 Lateral track right continues and the following superimposition fades in:

> Co-Production
> "Filmartic" Marcel Ichac
> FILMS DU CENTAURE
> Producteur delegue Paul de Roubaix

Superimposition fades out. Track stops, camera pans
slightly right past the tops of two trees in the foreground
and zooms forward to an ELS view of the bridge in the
center of the frame (soft drum roll) with bare trees on
the left and right. The small figure of the body hangs
from the bridge. (Drum roll ends.)

Fade out   (24

CRITICISM OF THE FILMS

LEWIS JACOBS

From
The Rise
of the American Film

The spirit of the time changed, and as American ex-
perimenters grew more familiar with their medium they turned
further away from the expressionism of the Germans and the
naturalism of the French to the heightened realism of the Rus-
sians. The impact of Russian films and their artistic credo,
summed up in the word "montage," was so shattering that they
wiped out the aesthetic standards of their predecessors and
ushered in new criteria. The principle of montage as presented in
the films and writings of Eisenstein, Pudovkin, and especially
Vertov, became by 1931 the aesthetic guide for most experimental
filmmakers in the United States.

Among the first films to show the influence of Soviet technique
was a short made by Charles Vidor called "The Spy" (1931–1932),
adapted from Ambrose Bierce's story, "An Occurrence at Owl
Creek Bridge." "The Spy," like "The Last Moment," revealed
the thoughts of a doomed man. But unlike the earlier film, which
used a flashback technique, "The Spy" used a flash forward. It
depicted not the recollections of the events of a past life, but the
thoughts of the immediate present, projected as if they were taking
place in reality instead of in the mind of the doomed man.

Reprinted by permission of the publisher from Lewis Jacobs, *The
Rise of the American Film: A Critical History with an Essay,
Experimental Cinema in America, 1921-1947* (New York: Teach-
ers College Press, 1968; copyright 1939, 1947, 1967 by Lewis
Jacobs). pp. 555–556.

158

The picture opens with the spy (Nicholas Bela) walking between the ranks of a firing squad. Everything seems quite casual, except for a slight tenseness in the face of the spy. We see the preparations for the hanging. A bayonet is driven into the masonry, the rope is fastened, the command is given, the drums begin to roll, the commanding officer orders the drummer boy to turn his face away from the scene, the noose is placed, the victim climbs to the bridge parapet. Now the drumbeats are intercut with the spy's beating chest. Suddenly there is a shot of a mother and child. At this point the unexpected occurs. The noose seems to break and the condemned man falls into the river. He quickly recovers and begins to swim away in an effort to escape. The soldiers go after him, shooting and missing, pursuing him through the woods until it appears that the spy has escaped. At the moment of his realization that he is free, the film cuts back to the bridge. The spy is suspended from the parapet where he has been hanged. He is dead.

The escape was only a flash forward of a dying man's last thoughts, a kind of wish fulfillment. The conclusion, true to Bierce's theme, offered a grim touch of irony.

In style "The Spy" was highly realistic. There were no camera tricks, no effects. The actors, who were nonprofessional, used no makeup. The sets were not painted flats nor studio backgrounds, but actual locations. The impact depended entirely upon straightforward cutting and mounting and showed that the director had a deep regard for Soviet technique.

DISCUSSION QUESTIONS

1. Look up the meaning of "montage" in a book on film technique, determine Jacobs' use of the term, and apply the term to "The Spy."

2. Jacobs calls "The Spy" "highly realistic" in style and states that there were no camera tricks or special effects. Do you agree?

JAMES M. WELSH

The First "Occurrence" on Film:
Charles Vidor and Ambrose Bierce

The first cinematic rendering of Ambrose Bierce's "An Occurrence at Owl Creek Bridge" was attempted by the Hungarian-American director, Charles Vidor, on the threshold of his Hollywood career in 1932. The film, variously titled "The Bridge" and "The Spy," shows considerable promise; but the creative potential it demonstrates was not, unfortunately, to be consummated in Vidor's later work, which included excursions into melodramatic sensationalism (*The Mask of Fu Manchu*, 1932), biographical and nostalgic sentimentalism (*A Song to Remember*, 1945, and *Love Me or Leave Me*, 1955), and a number of other competent but easily forgotten and generally undistinguished vehicles. At the end of his career, the year before his death, he returned to a substantial literary source, making the film version of *A Farewell to Arms* (1958). Vidor directed at M-G-M, Paramount, Warners, RKO, and Columbia, where he gained a reputation as Harry Cohn's "most serviceable director" during the 1940s.[1] While at Columbia he directed Rita Hayworth in *Gilda* (1946), a movie that has been called "a masterpiece of *Kitsch*."[2] No one, to my knowledge, has seriously proposed Charles Vidor as an *auteur* director.

James Welsh, an Assistant Professor of English at Salisbury State College, teaches film courses and writes for film journals.

[1] Bob Thomas, *King Cohn: The Life and Times of Harry Cohn* (London: Barrie and Rockliff, 1967), p. 248.

[2] Charles Higham and Joel Greenberg, *Hollywood in the Forties* (London & New York: Zwemmer-Barnes, 1968), p. 10.

One should remember, however, that Hollywood has not always brought out the best in foreign directors who have emigrated there. Even Fritz Lang, for example, after an initial period of brilliance on California soil, had descended by the 1950s to the depths of *Moonfleet;* and Max Ophuls has the dubious credit for *Caught.* When in 1931, at the age of thirty-one, Vidor undertook "The Bridge," his vitality and inventiveness had not yet been dulled by the accommodating demands of the Hollywood industry that would later relegate to him demeaning and hackneyed assignments of the order of *Johnny O'Clock.* The relatively unspoiled Vidor brought to his task of treating Bierce's Civil War story a number of effective techniques—editing tricks that strongly suggest the considerable influence of the Soviet silent cinema, double and triple exposures (see shot 40 in the shot analysis, for example) that recall the best work of Murnau and Dupont, and compositorial arrangements that are redolent of Fritz Lang's accomplishments at Ufa–Universum Film, A.G., Germany's largest and most influential studio. (The rigid arrangement of the marching soldiers surrounding the anxious prisoner at the beginning of "The Bridge" calls to mind Lang's trudging automatons in *Metropolis,* for example.)

"The Bridge" is purely visual and demonstrates the highest accomplishment of the silent film in the way it is able to tell a story effectively and aesthetically by undiluted action. The continuity of movement is never interrupted by subtitles. The only verbal message that is conveyed comes very late in the film (shot 112), when the camera pauses momentarily on a piece of paper upon which the word "Spy!" is written. As in the case of F. W. Murnau's *The Last Laugh* (1925), no title cards are used, and none are necessary. The action is narrated visibly as the camera itself probes the depths of a disturbed man's psyche and perfectly conveys his last thoughts and feelings. Like *The Last Laugh,* Vidor's "The Bridge" may be considered "cine-fiction in its purest form."[3]

[3] Paul Rotha and Richard Griffith, *The Film Till Now: A Survey of World Cinema* (London: Spring Books, 1967), p. 100.

"The Bridge" has been called "realistic," even though its central portion records the fantasy of a condemned man's final thoughts. The precedent for cinematic realism in the United States had been established by King Vidor during the 1920s, before Charles Vidor had established himself as a Hollywood director. King Vidor's last silent film, *The Crowd* (1928), predates and anticipates the Italian Neo-Realist movement by some fifteen years both in method (taking the camera out into the real world, recording the actions of ordinary people, and utilizing nonprofessional and unknown actors) and theme (the pathetically limited career and accomplishments of the common man). Part of *The Crowd* was shot on location in New York City with the camera hidden in a truck, capturing the interaction of the film's central characters with "real" people in the street scenes. As Lewis Jacobs reminds us (see the excerpt from *The Rise of the American Film*, p. 159), Charles Vidor's "The Bridge" was shot entirely on location, capturing and creating a deceptively natural atmosphere. The actors were not professionals, and their natural appearance was not altered. The central figure, Peyton Farquhar in Bierce's story, was played by Nicholas Bela, who was not an established professional actor.

The film thus begins and ends with a heightened sense of outer reality, the reality that is thrust upon us so forcefully as the drum-roll montage that introduces the fantasy sequence is repeated to make the necessary transition back to the actual hanging. The fantasy sequence itself, however, can be said to transmit a kind of inner reality in the way it convincingly records and puts the viewer in sympathy with the doomed prisoner's frame of mind. The distortions, deceptively countered against the natural setting, are a logical extension of psychological reality.

"The Bridge" begins with images of disciplined and controlled motion and confinement. The soldiers march evenly, rank and file, enclosing the prisoner, whose eyes betray his anxiety and desperation. Efficiently and unemotionally the soldiers make their preparations for the hanging. The setting established, the noose is made ready; the captive's situation would seem to be a hopeless one. But the human spirit yearns for escape; from the viewpoint of the desperate man—which almost imperceptibly becomes that of the viewer himself—the situation cannot be absolutely hopeless. What if the rope should break?

The montage sequence that follows this preparation just as Farquhar is about to be executed is nicely done. The superimposed images of the beating drum (shot 40), momentarily imposed over Farquhar's face and momentarily suggesting the face of a clock, the drumsticks arranged like the clock's hands—these images stress the urgency of Time for a man whose time is about to run out. The image also prepares us for what is to follow: Time in the film is about to be warped, extended, drawn out, and nearly stopped.

The symbolism controlling that drumroll montage (shot 40) is consistently organized and coherently structured so as to make the necessary transition into the memory of the doomed man. The image of the military drum is superimposed over Farquhar's face; then the image is shifted to a position directly above his heart (from clockface to heartbeat—we can almost hear the pulsating rhythms of time, heart, and drum) and blends into that of a drum beaten by his child. The montage then goes on to capture the sprinting psyche of a frantic mind trying desperately to maintain its hold on the existential reality that is about to shatter.

The shots conveying the frantic moments that immediately follow are brief, numerous, and fleeting, a complex montage demonstrating the disjointed thoughts of a man about to die. Then, however, the rope snaps, and escape apparently becomes a possibility. The camera goes subjective as Farquhar begins his swim to apparent safety. The pace quickens as the illusion of motion is created when the camera plunges through the water. This effect, I believe, could have been better conveyed if the camera had remained consistently subjective until Farquhar reaches the safety of the shore. As it stands we see the action subjectively one moment, then objectively as Farquhar comes up for air. On the other hand, the visual effect works subjectively in two ways: The racing water could be seen from two very different subjective points of view—that of a man swimming through it, or that of a man falling towards it after having been prodded off the side of the bridge. Hence it is both real and unreal, as seen from either psychological perspective.

Once he has arrived at the shore and is apparently out of the reach of his enemies, Farquhar begins his race homeward. The takes, by comparison, become longer, the atmosphere more deceptively relaxed as he pauses to pluck a sprig of flowers (shots 74–75). We are therefore lulled into the notion that he has been saved. But that noose remains around his neck, a visual reminder, ready to pull him back to external reality.

In Farquhar's journey down the road Vidor successfully shows the exuberance of a man who has presumably escaped death. The mannerisms are extreme, and his exuberance is curiously demonstrated through a number of military gestures (shot 76): he marches, a branch propped riflelike on his shoulder; he salutes, casually and derisively. The mocking gestures in his exuberant moments also provide an existential assertion of character that the emotionless and mechanical military execution had deprived him of: these may be taken, then, as sublimated gestures of defiance. Thereafter he runs along the road, with the superimposed images of his wife and child reminding us all the while of what it is he's running toward as his thoughts mislead us.

This image, an exuberant man racing down the road of life, filled with confidence and joy, but in fact about to be cut off from happiness that is all too transitory, fleeting, and illusory—this image is an all-too-common one, and parallel examples at once come to mind: the final shot of Dovzhenko's *Earth* (1930), for example, shows a man alone on the road, slightly tipsy, happy, and exuberant, and about to be cut down by a sniper's bullet. The successful truckdriver in Henri-Georges Clouzot's *The Wages of Fear* (1953), having delivered a load of nitroglycerine over an impossibly perilous route and having proved himself the best driver in the Western hemisphere, in a moment of careless exuberance waltzes his now empty truck off the road and down the mountainside. The juxtaposition of confidence and happiness against senseless destruction and death cannot fail to make an emotional impact.

In Vidor's film the illusory central portion is carefully anticipated. The plausibility of a rope's breaking so easily is questionable, to say the least; but the viewer is sympathetic, and the illusion created is an acceptable form of wish fulfillment. We want to see Farquhar reunited with his family, and we forget the implausibility of the broken rope until, at the end, we, like Farquhar, are pulled up by it and jolted back into reality.

In the central portion itself it is perfectly logical to suppose that Vidor is working a variation on the somewhat clichéd notion that, at the very point of death, one's whole life passes before his eyes. So considered, the drumroll montage could easily suggest that the young boy beating the drum may be Farquhar himself as a youth, and that Farquhar's mind is racing back into the recesses of his own past. From this point of view the final shots (101 and 103), when the woman and child (i.e., himself and his mother) turn their backs and move off ghostlike, make consistently good sense: the character, unable to escape through his memory, is in fact about to escape his predicament—and the larger predicament of the human situation—through death.

Vidor's interest, then, has focused upon the deceptive element of phantasmagorical escape as created in the mind of a man who knows he is about to die. The film succeeds in achieving this effect.

DISCUSSION QUESTIONS

1. Welsh comments on the inconsistency in camera point of view during Farquhar's swim to safety. If the camera were consistently subjective, we would gain the illusion of motion, but what would be lost?

2. Welsh notes the ambiguous nature of the drumroll montage: Farquhar projects himself into the future; he regresses into the past. Can Vidor have it both ways? Does the apparent ambiguity detract from the theme of the film? Explain.

JACK SHADOIAN

The Question of Technique in
"An Occurrence at Owl Creek Bridge"

For openers, I'll make a friendly gesture and dis-
remember all knowledge of Ambrose Bierce's story. That'll cut
out a lot of enlightened fussiness about how film perverts the
literature it feeds on. That's more of an inevitability than a
cultural disaster anyway. So why don't we be properly virtuous
and talk about film as film, like they say.

Since there's all kinds of film, let's dump this one quickly into
some available category so we know what kind of thing we'll be
talking about. You know it won't come to your local drive-in with
The Flesh Eaters and Mondo Whip-o. This is serious stuff—severe,
unvulgar, done with integrity. Besides, who but a true artist would
have the incorruptibility or expressive need to take on an undis-
tributable project like a half-hour film and see it through? It's
financially risky to be on the side of the angels, but the personal
satisfaction goes a long way, and there are Film Societies and individual spokesmen among serious film students who'll help out.
And you'll most likely see "An Occurence at Owl Creek Bridge"
at a film society, club, or on the university circuit as a bonus
accompanying some intellectually irreproachable main feature.
But Enrico's film really straddles the line between a feature film
and a short subject. Also, since it avoids both the (almost) ines-
capable narrative focus of the standard fiction film and the kinky
deviations (in both subject matter and technique) of the "under-
ground," we can maybe get by calling it a kind of cinemasong or

Jack Shadoian is Assistant Professor of English at the University of
Massachusetts, Amherst, and has reviewed records for Rolling
Stone.

lyric. But, a lyric whose rapturous center is diffused, and possibly confused, by a story line. You sing along, but you follow the bouncing ball, too.

I say "lyric" for want of a better word, since "An Occurrence at Owl Creek Bridge" is strangely depersonalized. I see no self-expressive impulse in either content or style. The intellectual sense of the film is elusive, and meanings evaporate as fast as the mind can conceive them. We wonder not merely what it means (one could whip up potential themes lickety-split) but also why it was made, what its fundamental purpose might be. I'm left with the unhappy conclusion that the film is a museum piece, a showcase for technical powers that has only a weak success in arousing our feelings or changing our minds, but a strong success in making us admire its skill. In due time, someone will tell you it's a masterpiece. I myself think it's an empty (if frequently stunning) exercise. In either case, you'll want some convincing.

"An Occurrence at Owl Creek Bridge" begins impressively with a series of images that suggest a skill beyond mere professionalism—there's inspiration as well. The mist mixing through the mist and foliage is captured with starkly mysterious angles. The camera penetrates the scene as though it holds a mystery. The editing implies a calm, though an illusory one. The bridge is brought closer and closer, leading into its importance. There's a beautiful passage where the camera pans in one direction and the motion of the soldiers filing across the bridge is choreographed in a slower countermovement to the pan. It is done with an exceptionally harmonious smoothness, the result of careful work and a fine attentiveness to mood and atmosphere. I suppose, as well, that the attempt is to create the efficient orderliness of military procedure. Intimations of an accompanying severity are borne out, however, by a sudden close-up of a man to be executed, which breaks the false harmony, and by the soundtrack with its naturalistic insistence on picking up every sound distinctly—the clank of weapons, the sharp report of boots on the wooden bridge, noises from the river and the woods. These are thrown into greater prominence by the verbal silence and are allowed to exist as though in ironical counterpoint.

The hangman, perhaps too predictably, is seen at an ominous

angle from below. This shot is peculiar, for it cannot represent the point of view of the bearded man awaiting execution (he is at a different level). This is, I think, a pointed instance of the conflicting impulses which threaten the film's coherence and are finally responsible for our dissatisfaction. Here it is the camera, and not the situation itself, that's providing the viewer's fears and emotions (later it will switch to representing the prisoner's point of view). A camera needn't be objective in all instances of course, but here it is a little too quick to melodramatize and somewhat truant in providing information. It's difficult to create suspense in a vacuum where no sympathies or facts are in play, where there is neither knowledge of a specific kind nor implications of moral metaphysical mood. On such occasions a viewer may feel unduly manipulated, may feel that his susceptibility to mood pure and simple is being too flatly exploited.

The problem may reside in a creative impulse that is at odds with the vehicle chosen to convey it. A viewer perceives the situation as narrative, while Enrico's absorption in mood and thematic implications causes him to neglect that. Mood and theme may well in the end be more important, but here they preempt the "occurrence" that must involve us before mood and theme can register. "An Occurrence at Owl Creek Bridge" is bound by a story, after all, and we see it (at least at first) as a story—but how it works as a story is the one aspect Enrico overlooks. The initial situation is a frame or *raison d'etre* for the main illusory sequence, but if it is to set us up for what follows, simply casting a spell on our eyes is not enough. Because he sees it as ancillary to the film's principal concern, Enrico misconstrues this initial situation and/or uses it to serve a function it is unsuited for. Having inadequate context, this opening sequence goes on a bit too long and suspense is dissipated rather than increased. What is visually arresting becomes obviously so. We are audience to a "poetic" cinema that is sacrificing its apparent goal—getting us absorbed in the situation—to an excessive stylistic mannerism. Means to an end become an end in itself, and our involvement gets displaced from interest in the event to an appreciation of the observation of the event. This is not good storytelling or even good singing, but an academic peroration that ultimately subverts the primary focus of interest.

An accomplished treatise, yes, but so far not an absorbing movie.

As the moment of doom appoaches the prisoner is given a flashback of his wife and home. (Suspense, as I've claimed, has slackened due to a technical overelaborateness. The continual panning is too intrusive and images like the sun coming up over the woods are too heavily savored as dazzling in themselves, with the result that a *sense* of mystery has given way to the actual mystery of what the hell is going on.) It's done in slow motion, presumably to emphasize an attempt to arrest time and to savor the moment. It works, as does the sharp recall to reality with the first spoken words in the film: "Take his watch." When I say it "works," however, I mean only that our eyes have no impulse to wander. Look at it another way and it doesn't seem to work at all, especially in retrospect. The prisoner's home is large, lush, conspicuously affluent, his wife is a lovely aristocratic woman, and he himself is attired like no Confederate soldier or poor rogue, but like a rich civilian. The watch is an expensive one and the Yankees are quick to appropriate it as a spoil of the war. There's enough material here to develop in any number of directions (as we watch, we reasonably expect it to be), and possibly lead towards a characterization. But nothing is done with it, as if to imply that nothing need be. Why then the loaded details? I think Enrico carries some assumptions too far, and various elements that could generate meaning and feeling are left fuzzy. Perhaps the details are intended as mere accessories to realism, as means of establishing verisimilitude. If so, our hunger for information nonetheless transforms them into potential clues for meaning, precluding their imagistic neutrality. The goal(s) of the film momentarily fall into a confusion. The responses of a viewer move in several directions and often bump into each other.

There's a close-up of the prisoner's trembling face, and then they hang him. He plunges into the river, snapping what tension has been built up. The camera follows him underwater. It's here that the film begins a new movement and a new emphasis. Enrico's apparent aim is to make what follows both real and unreal, to reveal that it is not only an illusion triggered by the prisoner's desire to live but also the reality we would have it be in so far as, being mortals, we would willingly lend energy and sympathy to any struggle for life. This is no easy task, and Enrico makes some wise choices. He gets by with letting the rope break because our collective desire as audience is to have death averted. Complaints of unlikelihood would be forestalled by our instinct for survival. But Enrico can't simply continue in this way. We can have our fantasies gratified for just so long. Instead (and it's a wise decision), he does several things that make the sensation of illusion and reality perpetually questionable. While our wish to believe is being fed by images that nourish it, it is also put under considerable strain. When Peyton Farquhar hits the water he goes down, down, down, down, unnaturally far down. Nothing is spelled out, but this is a descent into the subconcious, a fantasy world. So when he comes up, up, up, it is as though from an unreal region, a region that will allow extensions of possibility that would otherwise tax our willing suspension of disbelief. Thus the film sets us up for what follows and pursues what appears to be its main interest or theme: a visualization of the relationship between "real" reality and what exists in the mind, thereby forcing an audience to experience the sensation and quality of life in a different way.

Peyton Farquhar stays underwater a painfully long time, too long for us to feel he can survive. But because we want him to, and because he wants to (as the film later makes clear), we extend our credulity. More than that, we physically experience his struggle. We see him thrash and free his hands and eventually surface, as an expensive boot floats away. The emphasis provided by the camera is not one of horrible anguish but a kind of gracefulness, a water ballet of odd lyricism given the event which precipitated it. We expect a rough, animal energy, but the smoothness is appropriate to optimistic fantasy. Still, there are problems. Since we don't know who this character is or what he's done we don't particularly care what happens to him except on the level of an automatic instinct for self-preservation. Enrico's reliance on visual pyrotechnics blinds him to certain inevitabilities in a viewer's response. We may well be susceptible to the poetry, but we also wonder about elements (of no interest to the filmmaker) provoked by a narrative. The character is too particularized to function as Everyman, and his situation is peculiar enough to warrant a more helpful context. This is not Man facing Death—or if it is, the presentation backfires.

By the end of the film, when Peyton Farquhar actually and permanently hangs, we realize without a doubt that every frame of film from the moment he hits the water represents a last-minute crowding of emotions. The images are all visually descriptive of emotions. The actual hanging is the climax and, one hopes, the scene in which the meaning of prior events and images will crystallize. But it is not such a scene, but one of mere surprise, a sudden wrenching from subjectivity to objectivity that illuminates nothing. It reinforces our suspicion that the film is not working coherently. Instead of an emotional climax we are supplied with a theoretical proposition that the prisoner was a victim of his own illusions.

While a prose narrative can move freely within its story to raise theoretical questions, can supply ironies and shifting points of view and subtle perspectives that will enlarge or specify or modify the meaning of the events it is describing, a film that takes such liberties is more likely than not to get into a mess because its power of *present* actualization is so fundamental that any prolonged tampering with it is apt to result in clumsiness, come out not as valid illumination but plain trickery. So here we are not instructed or moved, but jarred, stupefied. This effect might be acceptable if our expectations were being developed towards an arbitrary sensationalism. But the film is obviously working to achieve an intellectual substance and focus, is almost stiff-jointed in implying that what it's doing is bristling with meanings.

At any rate, what starts out as a coldly brilliant *tour de force* gets progressively weaker. The prisoner surfaces from underwater with a loud, convincing gasp (the film's last unqualifiedly fine moment). Finding himself alive, he starts communing with a Nature that we're to understand he (and by extension, us) has taken too much for granted. His new appetite for life dictates an understanding of the mysterious quality of life itself, what it is to be living, however minute or inconsequential (from a human viewpoint) most organisms are. To underline this activity, the pace of the film slows almost to a halt. The ending, of course, explains the unnaturalness of this. In the meantime we share his wonder, are consumed by the same curiosity to the extent of forgetting about his executioners. Leaves and spiders seem to have a wondrous life, as wondrous as our own. Narratively, however, the situation is inevitably awkward despite all efforts of technique, and the awkwardness is compounded by having Nature sing a flaky folk song to her new convert—with a "cool" jazz background no less. The film is short enough to allow such a glaring error of taste to remove it from serious consideration. Some anticipation ought to have been made as well of the film being so inescapably dated by the music. Even assuming the music may please, the whole episode nonetheless belies Enrico's willingness to curtail the natural momentum of events, to abolish an established rhythm in order to theorize abstractly. For my money, abstract theorizing is more often than not inimical to film, accounting for impossibly arid stretches in the films of even first-rate directors like Bergman and Godard. It's pretty dumpy here, too.

Finally, there's a shot from the bridge, and although time seems to have been weirdly suspended, we have little trouble rejoining the action. The prisoner swims and ducks the bullets, trying to escape. The shots increase, and a cannon goes off. Once again, in contradiction to the realistic surface of the images, we sense a strangeness and a developing absurdity—a cannon shooting at one man? Maybe we're to infer, looking back from the conclusion, that the fear of death is projecting an exaggerated self-importance, a swift and extreme paranoia (possibly connected to a sense of guilt?—he is being hanged for something). Also, the soldiers on the bridge appear to him as surreal, twisted shapes, inhabitants of some imaginative hell. He eventually gets caught by rapids and is deposited on a sandy bank, alive. After a small fit of happiness, he relaxes enough to notice the sun in the trees, and flowers. You'll recall that at this point the music steals in again. But a full encore of that silly business is prevented by a crack of cannon—a reminder of time closing in—that sends him running off into the woods. Life is glorious, but he has discovered its glory too late. He runs and runs, with a speed and an endurance just barely credible—we again have to will it to be so. The music is now a steady drumroll, and the camera tracks along with uncommon smoothness. The studied gracefulness of this section is again indicative of dream. By now, though, I find the technical virtuosity (albeit still serving its purpose) too self-consciously highlighted and more distracting than ever.

The prisoner suddenly breaks through wilderness to find himself on a solacing (protective) straight road lined with civilized, geometric trees. As he runs down the road, the camera constructs a compositional triangle. He runs from a small apex of light (in the background) towards the wide base of the triangle in the foreground. He falls, rests, and on worn feet, gets up and resumes walking as darkness settles. Now, from behind, we see he's walking towards a black tunnel, an illusion of perspective formed by the trees over-hanging the road and by the camera placement. This probably signifies a failing grip on his illusions—the death he would escape is there after all. But he has a flash, and the light becomes radiant. It's a clearing, then home sweet home. His gracious, lovely wife is gliding to meet him, smiling with joy. Her routine movements are transformed by his urgency to relish them into an exquisite delicate-ness, and his home into a paradise of verdant civilization. He rushes furiously towards her, arms outstretched, but the camera records the futility of his effort. The short distance is too far; he doesn't make any ground, seems, in fact, to be retreating with each surge forward. What the camera has made us feel all along is asserting itself; it can't really be. In a final jolt of desire he reaches her, touches her, and with a sudden croak, hangs. The camera shows him hanging. Then the brutality of the exposure fades as the woods enclose the event. The camera retreats, panning a slow circumference of the setting, circling eventually back to the bridge to show a patrolling sentry in long shot calmly and peacefully going about his duties. The credits appear, notifying us of an accumulation of honors, including first prize at Cannes.

"An Occurrence at Owl Creek Bridge" is not a film without good moments. Many of its images have remarkable staying power and the camerawork never falters in quality. I feel, however, that the project was ill-conceived. It was perhaps too literary to begin with, its drive towards fantasy too shackled by thematic obligations. One typically feels that it's always a matter of surmounting problems in the script, that we are being given a series of solutions rather than the creative inspiration that is made possible by a script that allows for improvisational flexibility. The cross between lyric and narra-tive, instead of producing wonderful results, largely creates problems. A film like Bruce Baillie's *To Parsifal* has a pure lyrical impact be-cause it clearly disdains any narrative requirements. It is free to be a poem. This one isn't. Enrico's film straightjackets itself and its only resource is a technical impeccability. It has that, but not much else. The inevitable is made diagrammatic and the diagram is dressed up with a scintillating aesthetic silk. Creative vigor has been directed not outward towards discovery but inward towards a fastidious decoration. The character does not end up representing us, as we must presume is intended. His experience remains idiosyncratic because it is so much the camera's and so little his. The film falls victim to its own good taste and high skill because given a fragmented conception these are the means by which any kind of *whole* impact can be achieved. This is what *it* is involved in, and this is what we get involved *by*. It's one thing to be impressed, another to be satisfied. You know how sometimes you can see a movie and it's like a big steak you can live on for a week, a month, how you have no urge to see another until you've properly digested it? I couldn't live an hour on "An Occurrence at Owl Creek Bridge." All it does is to whet my appetite for something solid.

Still, proficiency as such is not to be despised; one ought to make movies competently, if at all. Since "An Occurrence at Owl Creek Bridge" is both well-made and brief, I think it can perform good service as a film to be studied by budding filmmakers. It shows a number of purely technical problems solved with enviable professionalism. Any study of it from this perspective would be profitable. I'm not nearly as confident that wrangling over its meaning or emotional impact would be quite as rewarding, and I don't think its few wisps of genuine poetry would survive that kind of a strain. Perhaps, also, it can be a demonstration model to instruct on the hazards of adapting literature to film (a topic outside the scope of this essay). It falls short, however, of being a totally satisfying movie experience.

DISCUSSION QUESTIONS

1. On the basis of this essay, how would you define the "intellectual" film? Towards the end of the essay, the writer makes this comment: "For my money, abstract theorizing is more often than not inimical to film, accounting for impossibly arid stretches in the films of even first-rate directors like Bergman and Godard. It's pretty dumpy here, too." Do you agree? Does the writer's attitude here help to explain the tone of the first three paragraphs of the essay?

2. It is suggested that the central weakness of the film is due to an unresolved conflict between its narrative and its lyric elements. The writer goes on to note that the viewer will want to perceive the film as a narrative while Enrico appears to be absorbed with mood and thematic implications. What evidence can you find for such a view?

3. Shadoian considers the film to be a "museum piece" in that its technique is accomplished but self-conscious. He feels that the film could serve as a kind of text book on film technique for tyro filmmakers. Did you find the technique distracting?

4. What does the writer mean by noting that the camera is "a little too quick to melodramatize"? Does this opinion relate to the viewer's analysis of the characterization of Farquhar? With respect to this, the writer believes that Farquhar is "too particularized to function as Everyman" and "his experience remains idiosyncratic because it is so much the camera's and so little his."

5. The theme of the film is said to be "a visualization of the relationship between real reality and what exists in the mind." Do you agree with the writer that this theme accounts for the weakness of the film in that it is "too shackled by thematic obligations"?

6. Shadoian writes that the images detailing Farquhar's fantasy are "visually descriptive of emotions" felt at the moment before his death. Could any of the images be thought of as being visually descriptive of thoughts? The objective climax to the film is called "trickery" and un-illuminating because it does not "crystallize" the meaning of Farquhar's fantasy experiences. Do you agree with this?

7. What is your opinion of the writer's view that film's ability to actualize the present makes it difficult for En-rico to move about within the story in order to supply ironies, points of view, and perspectives that would serve to temper meaning as a prose narrative writer is able to do?

8. The guitar/vocal music is referred to as "a flaky folk song." Shadoian believes that this "glaring error of taste" in a film this short serves "to remove it from serious con-sideration." Can such a criteria, sometimes used in short story criticism, be applied to short films? Is it relevant in this instance?

JULIUS BELLONE

Outer Space and Inner Time: Robert Enrico's "Occurrence at Owl Creek Bridge"

The story of "An Occurrence at Owl Creek Bridge" is the occasion of the execution of a civilian violator of Union trespass law during the Civil War. The situation is obviously one of intrinsic drama. Surely there is hardly a more gripping subject of human interest than the execution of a human being. But highly charged material does not in itself assure a humanly meaningful expression of it. On the contrary, handled with shallow insight and skill, such material carries with it the risk of becoming nothing greater than a melodramatic entertainment. Strategically regarded, Robert Enrico's material is too easily grasped—too commonplace: we know too well already that man's appreciation of the beauty of life, the allness of life, becomes paramount when he is faced directly with the terror of death, the perception of void. The force of Enrico's film is in the dramatic rendering of that which is all-too-familiar.

Central to the success of the film is the conception of the character of Farquhar. The criminal charge against him does not inhibit the viewer from identifying with him; rather, his relative guiltlessness keys up identification. And without the distancing that results from a heinous act committed by a character exhibiting taints of a criminal personality, the viewer is overwhelmed by the accidental aspect of Farquhar's dying. The viewer is witness to a happenstance, a chance occurrence. On the whole, Farquhar is depicted as ordinary; nothing about him is imposing. Roger Jacquet, the actor Robert

Julius Bellone, Assistant Professor of English at Lincoln University, Penna., teaches film and has edited a volume of film criticism, *Renaissance of the Film* (1970).

Enrico chose, is short-to-medium in stature and does not have a theatrically expressive or heroic face. Jacquet's modest, quietly strong features project a sense of Farquhar's fullness of manhood—the suggestion of wholesome, healthy living. Clothing adds to the depiction of Farquhar. In contrast to the figures in military attire, his white blouse, brocade vest, and black cravat appear adroitly human. The early cut to Farquhar's wife and children, the inviting domestic scene that accents family love and joy, is a vivid reinforcement of the viewer's sense of Farquhar's elemental humanity.

For the viewer there is the clear emotional logic of the situation: Farquhar is about to die and we all must die. To become aware of Farquhar's situation is also to become aware of the uniqueness of time for man. From our perspective outside the film, we are appalled by the awesome gap between the indifference of the soldiers and the natural environment on the one hand, and Farquhar's feverish preoccupation with his existence on the other. What is taken for granted as a possibility is suddenly a felt actuality: the objective reality, the law of the universe, closes in on and annihilates subjective reality, the human essence. That perception of two different realities, of two different points of view confronting man—the objective will of the universe and the subjective reality of individual consciousness—is established early in the film as the conceptual framework within which dramatic meaning is created.

"An Occurrence at Owl Creek Bridge" consists of two actions or parts that determine its structure: the one action is the preparation and hanging of Farquhar; the other is Farquhar's imaginary escape sometime prior to his being hanged. (It should be remembered that the first action or part is not to be regarded entirely in terms of sequence; it includes the end of the film.) The artistic challenge to the filmmaker is to cinematically dramatize an overriding or prevailing sense of objective reality in the first action and of subjective reality in the second. Before discussing the film as a whole, it will be necessary to examine briefly how two different kinds of time function in the film, one for the preparation and execution of Farquhar and another for the unfolding of the drama in Farquhar's consciousness.

Film is a medium superbly suited for the manipulation of time. Unlike the stage, it allows total freedom from the time and space continuum. Basically the filmmaker has the means to present three different kinds of time. He may present actual time by simply not editing his footage, by making his film one long take. He may present "actual" time by editing out footage in such a way as to create the illusion of real time passing. (This, of course, filmmakers do most often.) And last, he may present psychological time by filming actions in time spans which do not fit a sense of clock measurement but which do reflect man's inner, psychological sense of time. The first part of "An Occurrence at Owl Creek Bridge" is presented in "actual" time. Robert Enrico cuts film segments and arranges them so that they convey the illusion of continuous action. As the dawn comes on, for example, the nearly imperceptible advancing of light—as from the morning sun's progress—contributes to the sense of unbroken time passing slowly. Thus, in the first ten minutes of the film, Enrico renders the half hour or so the soldiers wait for full sunrise before carrying out the military "ORDER." The second part of the film is presented in psychological time. Farquhar's imaginative enactment, the projection of his deepest fears and desires, must unfold in a span of time befitting the human intensity of his situation, the dreadful context in which he exists. From the standpoint of the psychological truth of time spans, then, it is entirely proper that the second part take up seventeen of the twenty-seven minutes of the film.

To discuss this cinematic work of art, we shall approach the film in terms of the two above-mentioned realities (objective and subjective) and, where desirable, specify contrasting elements such as point of view, rhythm, sound, images, etc. One must emphasize that such separations, however apparent and convenient in one sense, are by no means actual, since meaning in "An Occurrence at Owl Creek Bridge" emerges from both the creation and *interpretation* of its twofold structure.

In the first part camera positions are generally fixed and stable, and angles—more often than not—suggest an objective point of view. An initial shot in the film is a steady hold on the "ORDER" sign tacked onto a charred tree stump, the position to which the camera returns in the final shot of the film. The background of initial and final shots is an omniscient perspective of the setting. The background of the initial shot is a broad view of the setting in nature and is followed by a slow in and down tracking movement toward the center of the bridge, the stage of the human drama; and, likewise, the final shot is preceded by a countering back and return to the initial fixed position and all-encompassing angle. On the sound track birds of prey indifferent to the human perspective echo through the hollow. The intense "focusing" on the sounds of the birds abstracts them sufficiently for the viewer to recall them during Farquhar's eloquent personalization of nature, which is to come.

After tracking sentry, cannon, tent, and other props, the camera is maintained in relatively fixed positions on or near the bridge. Until Farquhar is tied, shots have the general effect of stressing his individuality and also the collectivity of the soldiers. There is, for example, the long shot of Farquhar followed by the shot of the line of uniformed men seen from his angle. Other shots, rapidly edited, study the ritual movements of the soldiers and underscore them as a way of warding off human emotion. During these shots, to express Farquhar's point of view, Enrico provides a sound track that magnifies and enlarges the significance of sounds, of any sound—the whirring of rope as it is pulled across the upper wooden member of the bridge, knots being tied, commands and responses, and footsteps. Also Farquhar's point of view permeates the stark image of the noose of the rope, shot upward, with only the neutral setting of sky surrounding it.

Thus far, Enrico has portrayed the external situation: Farquhar is about to die. Now he must create means of entry into the internal Farquhar. The shift of dramatic interest from the external to the internal Farquhar is developed in two series of shots. They occur between the binding and dropping of Farquhar—from the time he is fully bound, knotted, and placed in dropping position at the end of the plank until the transition to the imaginary action. Each series contains a very intimate close-up of Farquhar, and each builds to a climax.

In the beginning of the first series we see—from Farquhar's angle —the floating log which suggests the seeding of his fantasy of flight. We then see the slow tracking across the plank and the turning of the camera at a right angle up his body, ending in a close hold that frames his face and the vertical rope. With tension at a new peak, Enrico makes the brief cut to Farquhar's vision of his wife (another seeding, and now of the ultimate reach of his imagination). Hence, only after the level of his anxiety is at a visionary pitch does Enrico move inward, into the theatre of mind; that is, only after creating a monopolistic hold of the screen with images of outer or objective reality does he begin to crack it by cutting to the scene of Farquhar's wife—the beginning of the movement toward the total possession of the screen by the substance of Farquhar's hyper-consciousness. The flood of light on his wife's face registers poignantly his depth of feeling. Rhythmically, the scene, by its dreamlike movement, fore-shadows what is to come; musically, it introduces the first of two lyric themes in the film. As she moves toward him the scene is halted abruptly by the sound of his pocket watch, which momentarily mounts with pounding insistence to an obsessive, impressionistic beat. In the next and climactic shot, the last in the series, Farquhar is wakened and transfixed by the command to take his watch. In this context the watch, which plays music and keeps time, emerges as a symbol of his ambivalent perception, a concretizing image of the realities of living and dying, of tenderness and terror.

The second series of shots, those shots most immediately preceding the transition, are the filmic unit that builds the final peak of tension prior to Farquhar's imaginary action. The bridge shots, from fixed positions, cause a freezing of tension. With neither camera movement nor motion in the frame, the long shot and then the undershot of the bridge hold and reinforce emotion gathered from the cut to his wife and children and the shot of the musical watch. The most studied and moving close-up of Farquhar's face thus far appropriately follows. His face, intensely lighted, is excruciatingly anguished; lips tremble, eyes squint, sweat runs. Then from a high downward angle, we see the soldier stepping off the plank, unbalancing it, and Farquhar dropping with the rope secured around his neck. This climax ends the second series of shots. Next we see him underwater from a medium shot that also frames the rope broken and dangling.

In moving the action from bridge to water, Robert Enrico does not employ the usual devices to clarify a break in continuity from present to past or imaginary action. We anticipate cinematic punctuation when a shift of time, place and/or action is about to occur or when we think one is occurring. With the clearly illusory cut to

Farquhar's wife and the final action on the bridge, we feel that we have been alerted for some impending transitional signal. But none is given. Instead of the soft, releasing effect of the dissolve, a slow fading out and then in, for example, Robert Enrico moves the action from bridge to water in a fast, direct, and clear manner. In a strictly visual sense, there is no interruption of the impression of continuous, real time and action; that is, to first show Farquhar falling and then to show the broken rope as he is under water is to present action according to the sequential order of the time-space continuum.

Covertly, however, Enrico does effect the transition. There is, for example, the deep-throated gong on the sound track conjoining the bridge and water shots. Also, the water is exceptionally deep. Although these details might be considered too hidden for the viewer to take in consciously at the moment, thereafter Enrico does introduce images slightly confusing in their sequence. When Farquhar first surfaces, he observes biological life and only after does he attempt to flee his executioners. Besides sequential distortions, movements become faster and slower than they occur naturally. The transition is effected accumulatively, without anything being offered too directly to the viewer. It is a delicate cinematic effort to perpetuate viewer involvement—the sharing of Farquhar's desire to escape the tyranny of objective law. And it is more.

Given the duality of Farquhar's power of seeing, the blurred crossover fits exquisitely the nature of the relation between the real world and the imaginary action in the film. For although the second part of the film is dreamlike, it does not portray a dream. Farquhar's imaginary projection is caused by his being acutely awake—his "dream" is his reaction to intense contact with reality. The problem for Enrico was how to express visually Farquhar's extraordinary hold on the real world in his imaginary departure from it. And to a great extent his solution to the problem was stylistic. He avoided a pure dream style, the kind of possibility described by Bunuel:

> Motion pictures can best imitate the functioning of the
> human mind in a state of sleep. The film is like an invol-
> untary imitation of a dream. The images, just like in a
> dream, appear and disappear through fadeouts and black-

outs; time and space become flexible, they shrink or expand at will; chronological order and the relative values
of duration no longer respond to reality; the action of a
cycle is to last a few minutes or several centuries; movements accelerate delays.

Enrico employed only with great restraint this plastic freedom
allowed by the medium. In the second part, he tread a middle
course between the Scylla of realism (the first part) and the Cha-
rybdis of surrealism (the extreme possibilities described by Bunuel).
He made the second part as much like the first as possible, making
them distinct yet not separate from one another.

Through various techniques he manages to create a sameness of
cinematic style. While there is *apparent* continuity of action in the
film up to the very end, the actual hanging of Farquhar, there is a
corresponding stylistic unity throughout the film. In spite of the
mildly surreal detail in the imaginary action, the textural consis-
tency of the film absorbs and enfolds even the unrealistic movements and disjunctive relationships between movements, so necessary to the imaginary meaning.

An important element in Enrico's search for this total unity is
the harmonious use of artificial lighting. That early morning sunlight
affects consistently the appearance of nearly all objects in the film
is rather obvious. Yet the brightening of light objects, and the stressing of dark objects by contrast, is a small step beyond the realistic
suggestion of the natural light of the sun. Enrico creates a lumines-
cence that is subtle and unobtrusive in its presence and impression-
ism. The sun is dazzling, and the shining of it directly into the
lenses of the camera expresses and generates an atmospheric feeling
that is subduedly maintained from time to time throughout the film,
There is the radiant light on the water as Farquhar peers down at
the floating log, and there is the illumination that surrounds him as
he swims. The same luminous presence emanates from close-up sub-
jects: the facial lighting of Farquhar and of his wife, the glistening
spider, crystallike moisture beads, or Farquhar's bloody hand; lighting stressing the shimmer of leaves or the animation of a water snake.

Also significant as an element in the atmospheric oneness of the
film is the sound track. One does not hear the sound effects as

though they were intended as natural decor; they are too pronounced to be merely that. Rather they are heard as auditory imagery, as it were. To a greater or lesser degree, pending dramatic need, the sound track is impressionistic. As already mentioned, often real sounds in the first part amplify as if from Farquhar's point of view. In the second part, the surrealistic sounds of Farquhar underwater and then surfacing and the muffled sounds of voices and movements on the bridge are vivid auditory suggestions of his inner drama. But, as he swims away, such distortions tend to cease. Sounds of firing, of missiles in flight, and of water flowing then become dramatically important—and again distorted—by their extraordinary clarity and piercing volume. Such modulation and timing of sound assures our emotional vascillation (escape-death)—we are denied release, the relaxation of tension that purer fantasy would permit.

On the level of music, too, the sound track is a unifying component. It integrates artfully counterpointed martial and lyric elements. The drumming at the beginning of the film is repeated during Farquhar's cycles of running. As the drum beats underscore the accelerated—and then further accelerated—movement of Farquhar's flight through woods, the insistent watch beats are recalled. Lyrically, there is the highly emotive melody played briefly in the early cut to his wife and children; and there is a second, reinforcing lyrical motif, "I want to be a living man." The latter plays when he first surfaces and revels in the beauty of nature, and again plays after he emerges from the water. All of these musical elements culminate in the final sequence of the film.

Besides lighting techniques and sound effects used in such a way as to connect the two parts of the film, Enrico also relates the two parts through a continuity of images; persistent images from the first part reappear in the second in a manner that is psychologically compelling. As already indicated, Enrico does not create the second part in dream style; there is not a remote and phantasmagorical changing of images from reality to dream. Instead there is a fluid development of the two parts, a development that convincingly accounts for the close time relationship between the fantasy and the reality that triggers it. Static images assimilated by Farquhar during the real action transform, under the heat of his imagination, with dramatic force. For example, the double shot of Farquhar and the vertical rope on the bridge recurs as the first shot underwater, but now the rope is broken. (Incidentally, this repeated image indicates the time the director suggests the whole second action requires; namely, the time between the first double shot and the hanging.) On the bridge there is physical closeness between Farquhar and his executioners; from the water he looks up and the camera zooms close to his eye, the eyeball-to-eyeball effect. Isolated shots of the standing sentry, the cannon emplaced on the hillside, the line formation of soldiers, and the facial close-ups of the officer in charge and the attendant sergeant—all of which Farquhar studies—are images that recur clustered on or near the bridge as he is about to swim to his escape. As he is farther and farther from the source of his threat, the pace of his flight slows increasingly. The easing visual tempo indicates his progress in making recede the martial milieu and facilitates his bringing on, gradually, the domestic one. Images of helter-skelter running through woods give way to images of nature such as the serene colonade of trees. Now birds chirp peacefully. And, in the clearest surrealistic image thus far, the huge, massy gates open themselves—a transitional gesture that is a deft keying up to the dramatic level of the final scene of the imaginary sequence.

Charted on a graph, the buildup in "An Occurrence at Owl Creek Bridge" is one long ascending line, the building of dramatic tension through the interpenetrating realms of subjectivity and objectivity, generating feelings of longing and dread, confronting the reality of love and death. In the final scene of the imaginary sequence, Enrico distills the elements of the film that produce the keenest emotive effect—elements of lighting, sound, movement—in order to create a poetic consummation of the two parts of the film. Broadly speaking, this scene epitomizes the film as a whole: technically, it is cinematically formed by a heightened concentration of many techniques employed already; and thematically, it is the ultimate expression of Farquhar's overwhelming sensitivity. In it cinematic technique is put to the service of expressing the basic psychological fact that to retard or deny the gratification of human desire is to feed and escalate it.

Up to this point in the film, Robert Enrico employed tension-generating techniques of great potency, but sparingly, only as dramatic needs required the use of them. In this last scene techniques that create sharp psychological intimacy between subject and viewer —lyrical music, high intensity lighting, decelerated movement, and the extreme close-up—are employed fully.

A bar of the "Living man" melody plays as Farquhar's wife descends the porch stairs. As Farquhar sees her through leaves, he halts abruptly while the music modulates to the theme he associates with her in the early cut during the first part. As she walks towards him, her body movement, in time with the music, is emphasized by the rhythmic motion of her hooped skirt. While the two are coming towards each other the music plays with mounting volume; then it is replaced violently by its ubiquitous opposite—the final flourish of drums.

The dramatic impact of the facial close-ups as the film cross cuts repeatedly from her to him is greatly owing to the increasing concentration of artificial lighting. While the white dwelling is brightened and her white clothing is especially bright, the point of most intense light is her face, which is light-complexioned.

Her face grows in beauty, desire, and empathy as we are allowed to study the slow-motion formation of tearful smiling. Robert Enrico increases drastically the amount of time necessary for her to cross the lawn to meet Farquhar, and the amount of time required for her to form completely her smile. The retardation, excruciatingly wetting desire and longing, is further affected by the editing technique of having her descend the terrace steps four times. Simultaneously, Farquhar, as though he were impeded in advancing forward as one would be treading an escalator in reverse, is shown four times running toward her.

Hence while the scene is climactic in the obvious sense, it is also climactic in the degree and intensity to which Robert Enrico orchestrates these cinematic elements. This total implementation of powerful technical means is, again, correlative to meaning; the drama in the scene warrants the treatment given it.

The steady proximity of the real and unreal achieves its tightest juxtaposition and ultimate expression in the final shot of the scene. With it Enrico rivals his own invention of the blurred crossover at the beginning of the sequence. He gives the shot a simultaneous function by making it the last shot of the scene and also the first shot of Farquhar hanging. It portrays the simultaneous timing of the sensation of touch: imaginarily, the touch of love; actually, the touch of death.

There are no more close-ups of Farquhar. The medium for truth must be the long shot, the fully objective framing of Farquhar hanging from the bridge. The subject is static; the camera is fixed. Robert Enrico has dramatized the pathos of man's fate in the time-space continuum.

DISCUSSION QUESTIONS

1. Bellone notes that, given the nature of the film's material, the result could have been melodramatic. However, he believes that the characterization of Farquhar is central to Enrico's successful avoidance of melodrama. On the basis of the evidence offered, do you agree?

2. It is claimed that the film offers two different perceptions of reality, objective nature and a man's subjective view of nature. The writer suggests that the director distinguishes between these two perceptions of reality through point of view, rhythm, sound, camera movement or lack of it, and camera angles. Do the given examples convince you of this? Later in the essay, Bellone tells us that the film's stylistic unity links the objective and subjective perceptions of nature. Do the given examples convince you of this?

3. "One might say that there is and there is not a transition from real to imaginary action in 'An Occurrence at Owl Creek Bridge.'" How is this statement explained? Does it seem correct to you?

4. With respect to the very point of transition in the film, it is called "the most inventive transition from a real to an imaginary level in the history of the cinema." Explain the writer's reasons for such a statement.

5. Concerning the final sequence of the film, it is said that "cinematic technique here is put to the service of expressing the basic psychological fact that to retard or deny the gratification of human desire is to feed and escalate it." Explain the meaning of this statement and demonstrate its validity.

6. Bellone tells us that the cinematic elements in this scene also "create sharp psychological intimacy between subject and viewer." How is this accomplished?

7. Has Enrico "feelingly dramatized the pathos of man's fate in the time-space continuum"? Is that pathos the theme of the film?

GERALD R. BARRETT

Double Feature:
Two Versions of a Hanging

Ambrose Bierce's short story, "An Occurrence at Owl Creek Bridge," is a natural for a film adaptation and it has surely tempted many filmmakers over the years. The narrative is visual and objective, the action is exciting, and one of the themes, man in conflict with time, lends itself to cinematic representation. I have seen three adaptations of the story and have been told that a fourth version was screened on British television a few years ago. The earliest version seen, "The Bridge," was made by Charles Vidor in 1931–1932; another version, Robert Enrico's "An Occurrence at Owl Creek Bridge," won an Academy Award in 1963; finally, I remember seeing a third version on American television in the *Alfred Hitchcock Presents* series in the early sixties.

While all three films naturally differ in a number of interesting ways, certain differences between the Vidor and Enrico versions are of particular interest because they exemplify a polarity that has often been noted with respect to film technique. In some films, directors want the audience to consider the film intellectually; the audience is asked to think about what is being seen. If a director has this in mind, he will employ certain cinematic techniques that, in general, serve to distance the viewer from the actions on the screen so that he will not be so emotionally involved that he is unable to think about what he is seeing. One major tool will be the use of static camera shots. The static camera serves to distance us from what we are seeing in the sense that we perceive the actions as viewers and not as participants. In other words, our response to what we are seeing is objectified by the director's choice of technique.

In other films, directors do not want the audience to consider the film intellectually; the audience is not asked to think about what is being seen. If this is the case, a director will employ filmic techniques that will involve the viewer emotionally and allow him to suspend intellectual judgement. Here, one main tool will be the moving camera. When the camera pans, tilts, and, in particular, tracks, the viewer will tend to experience a greater sense of participation in the actions seen on the screen. He will become more emotionally involved, his responses will be much more subjective, and he will be inclined to think less about what he is seeing.

Two French films come to mind as examples of this objective-subjective polarity, Eric Rohmer's *My Night at Maud's* (1969) and Jacques Demy's *The Umbrellas of Cherbourg* (1964). Roger Greenspun has referred to the Rohmer film as a sophisticated adult film in which the characters sit around and talk about Pascal (*Rolling Stone*, June 10, 1971). *My Night at Maud's* has been successful with critics and general viewers because one gets a great deal of pleasure out of listening to and watching adults in lucid conversation. This film flatters the intelligence of the viewer, and Rohmer has cut his technique to the bone in order to do so. He does this, in part, by eschewing all transitions but the straight cut and by keeping his camera static. The camera moves when we get subjective shots of the protagonist in his car and it "moves" in the one zoom "track" late in the film, but that's about all. Rohmer wants the viewer to perceive the content on an intellectual level and his elimination of the moving camera is a correct aesthetic choice.

On the other hand, Demy's *The Umbrellas of Cherbourg* exemplifies the use of the moving camera as a means of emotionalizing the content of the film. Stanley J. Solomon has discussed the film from this viewpoint in the Winter 1965–66 issue of *Film Heritage*. Solomon lambasts it for its "torpid" editing, turgid physical movement, "trivial" plot, and mindless theme. Why then, Solomon asks, is it considered to be an energetic film and how is Demy able to get away with such poor material? The answer, as you may have guessed, is the director's use of moving camera techniques. The camera, in a sense, is the protagonist of the film as it almost constantly pans, tilts, and tracks in a veritable frenzy of movement. The viewer has no time to think about what is going on because he has become a participant in the action. Demy cleverly leads the viewer to suspend his intellectual judgement and the content of the film is thoroughly emotionalized.

Of course directors do not *have* to use the static camera for objective distancing or the moving camera for subjective participation, but most films tend to employ these techniques for the ends described. I'm sure that one could think of films in which objectifying techniques are used for subjectifying purposes and vice versa; but, on close inspection, it will be found that other cinematic techniques are used to undercut the sense of the basic polarity that has been noted. For example, in *La Passion de Jeanne D'Arc* (1927), Carl Dreyer's static shots of Jeanne and her interrogators tend to objectify the content of the film but his emphasis upon tight close-ups adds emotional impact. Conversely, his moving camera shots would tend to subjectify the content but he angles these or cuts them off before their logical point of conclusion so that the viewer is distanced from what he is seeing and seldom has a satisfying feeling of participation. Similarly, in Jean-Luc Godard's *Weekend* (1968), the famous tracking shot of the traffic-jam is objectified because the camera moves laterally past the action rather than towards or away from it. Godard further distances the viewer by consistently photographing the action in long shots. When we view the characters in close-up, our view is often obscured by trees, auto windshields, smoke, and backlit glare. Thus, it would be absurd to suggest that a director will always distance the viewer through the use of static shots, or that the moving camera is the only way to emotionalize the content, or that a film will be either wholly objective or subjective. In fact, most films are mixtures of objective-subjective techniques and most films are mixed with respect to the reasons for such techniques. However, a filmmaker's purposes become clear when we consider the aggregate result of his choices as they create an audience of viewers or participants.

While both the Vidor and Enrico versions of Bierce's "An Occurrence at Owl Creek Bridge" are mixtures of distancing and emotionalizing techniques, the films strike me as opposites because of the aggregate result of the technical choices. Vidor invites us to *think* about what we are seeing, while Enrico wants us to *emotionally respond* to the action of the film. Let us see if a close examination of each film buttresses this view. Furthermore, let us ask the question that logically follows: which approach is more appropriate to the similar content being presented?

Let's begin with a statistic on Charles Vidor's "The Bridge." Apart from the titles, there are 112 shots in the film. Only 19 are moving camera shots (mostly tracks), and the camera movement in shot 73 is of questionable value. Given the context of that shot and those surrounding it, the tilting camera may be the result of poor camera placement. The rest of the shots (static camera) either emphasize movement within the frame or image "movement" from shot to shot. Given the content, it is surprising that the film does not contain more shots in which the audience sees the world from the protagonist's point of view.

With respect to point of view, the film is divided into two parts. Prior to shot 40 (images of the civilian's family seen over the beating drum), the point of view is primarily objective. There are only nine shots in which we see things from the protagonist's perspective, and they are clustered from shots 12 through 27. In this section the civilian is watching the soldiers going about their preparations for a hanging, his hanging. Vidor could have involved us in the emotions the civilian is feeling by moving the camera in ways that would emphasize the civilian's heightened emotions. By doing so, our emotions would be heightened through a sense of participation; we would identify with the civilian, and his impending doom would be that much more terrifying to us. Instead, Vidor attempts to emotionalize the scene through rhythmic cutting of the images. Here is how it works: (10 MLS) the officer faces the drummer (five seconds); (11 CU) the civilian looks at the officer (2 seconds); (12 MLS) the officer walks to the side of the bridge (four seconds); (13 CU) the civilian watches (2 seconds); (14 MCU) the officer looks at the river (four seconds); (15 CU) the civilian watches (two seconds); (16 MS) the officer continues to look at the river (four seconds). By intercutting four-second images of the officer with two-second images of the civilian, Vidor hopes to get us involved in the emotions of the scene through editing rhythm. However, this fails, at least for me, for one major reason. While the short duration cuts of the civilian might create emotional tension, one becomes too aware of the mechanics of the 4–2, 4–2 editing. This is because there is more going on in the shots of the soldiers than in the shots of the civilian. One general rule for film rhythm is that the image should be kept on the screen only as long as it takes a viewer to respond to the image as the director desires. In the context of this portion of the scene, civilian reaction shots of more than two seconds would seem interminable. If Vidor had pared these shots to durations of one second or less, the mechanics of the editing may not have been obvious and we would have been more emotionally involved with what we were seeing. As they stand, the shots involve us intellectually but not emotionally. In shots 17 through 25, the action is more emotionally involving because the editing rhythm is more varied. By this time we have tired of the uniformity of the reaction shots of the civilian (11, 13, 15, 18, 20, 22, 24) and our emotional response is weakened further. Finally, Vidor's decision to almost constantly have the civilian in close-ups and the soldiers in medium shots adds to the mechanical feeling of the action.

After shot 40, the point of view is a mixture of objective and subjective shots; sometimes we see things from a viewer's perspective, sometimes through the civilian's eyes. All but one of the moving camera shots is in this section of the film, but the majority of these are third-person shots. However, since the moving camera tends to emotionalize content, the effect upon the viewer in this film should be roughly the same as a first-person shot. Unfortunately, the majority of Vidor's moving camera shots (found in 88 through 96), all tracks, fail to achieve the desired emotional effects. Back on land after eluding the soliders by swimming downstream, the civilian happily walks down a road with the camera tracking back in front of him (76). Suddenly, he fears that he is being pursued (79) and runs off into the woods. The combination of static shots, pans, tilts, varied angles, and mixed durations involves us in the man's flight through the trees and over the hills (80–87). But when the civilian begins to have visions of his wife and child while running down a country road (88–96), Vidor's problems begin. First of all, in spite of the superimpositions of the family over the empty road in the tracking shots (seen from the civilian's point of view), the aggregate effect is tedious because the shots are too mechanical. Shot 88 (MS) is an objective track of the civilian running down the road. Shot 89 (LS) is a subjective track of the road in front of him with superimpositions of his wife and child. This ping-pong effect (man running down road, empty road with superimpositions) continues for seven more shots without a change in the basic action. Again, the mechanics of the editing distances us from what we are seeing. Admittedly, the shot durations are varied and shot 95 breaks the pattern with a close-up of the family fading out and leaving an empty road, but the over-all effect is tedious. This is because the actions of the wife and child are unimaginative, and these superimpositions are not strong enough to take one's mind off the continual forward tracking shot of an empty road. The majority of the moving camera shots in the film do not give us a sense of participation; the best that could be said is that they distance us from what we are seeing and allow us to *think* about the action.

Vidor's most successful attempts at emotionalizing his content occur during the two dramatic high points in the film, the actual hanging (shots 43–52) and the transition from fantasy to reality at the end of the film (shots 100–109). Both sequences gain their ends through the rhythmic editing of static camera shots. All but one shot has a duration of three-quarters of a second or less and all but the first two shots are close-ups: shot 43 is a three-quarter second long shot of a soldier prodding the civilian off the wall; shot 44 is a medium low-angle shot of the falling civilian. The remaining eight shots are of the falling man, his wife and child, and the man at the end of the twisting and fraying rope. Here, Vidor is fairly successful in giving us a sense of the jumble of thoughts and emotions a person would experience under such a circumstance. The director heightens this effect by extending the duration of the action through editing. Given the context of these shots, Vidor's choice of camera placement and duration is also aesthetically correct. Shots 100–109 work in much the same way and obtain the same emotional effect. Shot 106 is of particular interest in that its duration (seven seconds) works as a kind of visual caesura between two clusters of short duration shots.

As mentioned earlier, the film is divided into two parts. The first part (shots 1–40) tends to have us view the action objectively, perhaps to suggest the depersonalized way the civilian is being handled by the soldiers. If this is so, Vidor would have been well-advised to eliminate the sheepish soldier (26), the sorrowing drummer boy, and the understanding officer (41). The sentimentality here detracts from the objective purity of the scene. The final shots of the film (111–113) revert back to an objective view of the action; but again, the sentimentality of shot 111 weakens the objective ending. The second part of the film (shots 41–110) emphasizes the subjective responses of the civilian to his experience; but Vidor's editing rhythms and moving camera shots seldom emotionalize the content. Thus, we tend to *think* about what we are seeing rather than to *emotionally respond* to what we are seeing. Let's conclude this consideration of "The Bridge" with another statistic. Rod Whitaker (*The Language of Film*, Prentice-Hall, 1970) has noted that "the average theatrical film of the fifties had about two hundred cuts per hour." Vidor's film (1931–1932) is eleven minutes long and contains one hundred and eleven cuts. Seventy-four cuts have a duration of four seconds or less. Given such rapid editing, it is curious that the film isn't more emotionally involving. However, to be fair to Vidor, one must remember that psychological responses to cutting rates and tempos change over the years.

I noted earlier that Godard's *Weekend* contains a tracking shot that discourages a sense of viewer participation because it moves laterally past the action rather than towards or away from it. Brian Henderson has written on this technique ("Toward a Non-Bourgeois Camera Style," *Film Quarterly*, Spring 1971) and distinguishes between lateral tracks that do not move in relation to the action within the frame, those that serve to "discover" fixed or moving objects in frame-space, and those that simply follow actions. While all three types of lateral tracks tend to distance us from the action, lateral tracks that move without reference to action within the frame are obviously more objective than those that are following action on a parallel line. Further, it follows that the distance between camera and object and the sense of depth between camera and object created by multiple planes or even lens lengths should also be taken into account.

Robert Enrico's "An Occurrence at Owl Creek Bridge" may be divided into five uneven parts; the first and last parts (shots 1–5 and 141–144) consist of moving camera long shots of the hilly landscape in the vicinity of Owl Creek bridge. With these shots, Enrico attempts to sandwich his account of a hanging between two highly objective visual sequences. Vidor attempted to do much the same in his opening and closing sequences, but Enrico is more successful. First of all, his decision to have camera movement in all nine shots allows the viewer to smoothly enter into and exit from an essentially emotional presentation. Secondly, the director's employment of lateral tracks in six of the nine shots gives the viewer an appropriate sense of discovery. Shots 2–5 give the effect of a single lateral track ending with a high-angle extreme long shot of the bridge seen through the trees far below. Shot 6 is a MCU of the lieutenant on the bank of the stream; in effect, the viewer has come down from his objective position high in the hills and is forced to participate in the ensuing action. Enrico has prepared us for this psychological "drop" into the valley with the downward diagonal camera motion in shot 2. Similarly, shots 143 and 144, lateral tracks, serve to pull us out of the action we have witnessed and remove us to a distant vantage point where we again discover the bridge in an extreme long shot; but this time a body is hanging from it. The difference between the two experiences of discovery is suggested by camera placement. When we first come upon the bridge at the beginning, we see it in the distance from a high angle. At the end of the film, our distance from the bridge is about the same, but the camera angle is roughly level with the bridge. In other words, while we are equally distant from the kind of experience we have seen presented, our sense of identification with the hanged man is such that we realize that death happens to us all. This is what Enrico wants us to discover at the end of the film. We remain in the valley.

While it has been said that the lateral tracking shots in this film allow us to discover the action rather than be totally alienated from it or involved in moving with an action within the frame, all three kinds of lateral tracks tend to distance us from what we are seeing. Stanley Soloman (see above) has written that the lateral track (as used by Antonioni in *Red Desert* (1964)) has the effect of involving us emotionally in the action because of the camera movement but distancing us from what we are seeing because we are moving laterally to the action. Using this idea as a clue to Enrico's meaning in the two sections under consideration, it is significant that the effect of the lateral tracks in the first section (1–5) is to lead us to the extreme long shot of the bridge from a point off in the woods and the effect of the lateral tracks in the last section (141–144) is to lead us away from the bridge to a point where we view it in the distance. We are purposely distanced from the action so that we may intellectually consider its meaning and we are taken to this point by moving camera shots, rather than static camera cuts, because Enrico wishes to retain the emotions of the action we have just watched. Finally, the camera pans in shots 141 and 142 are appropriate introductory movements to the final tracks because they smoothly blend into the tracks (same speed and direction) through perfectly executed dissolves, and they serve the same rhetorical ends as the downward diagonal in shot 2. At the end of the film Enrico does not want to take us out of the valley.

The third reason for Enrico's success in the first and last sections of the film is implicit in the above description of the nine shots—their formal symmetry. The film begins with a close-up of a burnt tree trunk and tilts up to a sign declaring that anyone found tampering with railroad bridges will be hanged. The first shot ends with a diagonal upward to branches and sky over which the title of the film appears. The second shot begins with a downward diagonal ending in a lateral tracking long shot of the woods. The next three shots (all long shots) continue the lateral track and the first section ends with a high-angle long shot of the bridge. This section runs about two and one-half minutes and the shots average out to around twenty-eight seconds. The last section begins with the shot (141) of the hanging man. This medium long shot zooms out to a long shot of the body, and the camera begins to pan right. At that point, the wording on the sign seen during shot 1 is superimposed. The camera continues to pan over the trees on the bank of the river and credits are superimposed. The next shot continues the pan and the superimposed credits and dissolves into the two last shots of the film, lateral tracks. After the superimposed credits are completed during the last shot (144), the camera stops tracking, pans right, and zooms in to a long shot of the bridge, seen from a great distance. The film's last section is similar to the first in many respects: all of the shots are moving camera set-ups, the sequence runs about two minutes, and the shots average out to around twenty-eight seconds. Further, this last part has its own built-in symmetry: shot 141—static, zoom, pan; 142—pan; 143—track; 144—track, pan, zoom, static. However, in contrast to Vidor's film, the formal organization reinforces rather than overwhelms.

Most of the action of the film, nearly twenty-three of the twenty-seven minutes, is placed within the objective enclosures of the first five and last four shots. The point of view of the inner three parts consists of a fairly complex mix of objective "viewer" and subjective "participant" shots. Many of the objective shots are emotionalized through the use of camera movement, but these shots have differing effects that are dependent upon the relationship between the camera and the object with respect to distance and angle. Interestingly, nearly all of the subjective shots are taken from Farquhar's point of view. We see the soldiers objectively; we seldom have a sense of identification with them because we seldom see the actions through their eyes.

Part two of the film begins with shot 6, a medium close-up objective shot of the lieutenant standing at the head of the file near one end of the bridge. It ends with shot 40, a low-angle objective long shot of the body falling off the bridge. (The body completes its fall in an objective low-angle medium long view near the the end of the film, shot 141.) Although Enrico has us see the action from vantage points on the bridge or near it, we experience most of the action in part two as viewers rather than as participants. While this could be said of the entire film, this section contains relatively fewer moving camera shots than any of the other parts. Here, Enrico couples "viewer" shots with static camera placement to emotionally distance us from the action. This narrative technique allows us to think about what we are seeing and we notice the contrast between the mechanical actions of the military preparation and the emotions of the prisoner. A closer look at the shots reveals just how well Enrico achieves this effect.

This section begins with two moving camera "viewer" shots of the military preparations off the bridge (6 and 7) and then cuts to a less emotional high-angle extreme long shot of the civilian being escorted onto the bridge. Shot 9 is a static close-up of the man's face, possibly from a subjective viewpoint of one of the soldiers. (Shots 13, 32, and 36 are the only other shots in this section that could be thought of as a soldier's subjective view, and all are static.) Shots 10 and 11 exemplify the way in which Enrico allows us to identify with the subjective reactions of the prisoner thereby emotionalizing the content. Shot 10 is a subjective moving camera view as seen by Farquhar. We (Farquhar) see the rope thrown over a timber overhead and then we look down to watch a soldier pulling the rope tight. The overexaggerated sounds emphasize that we are watching the action from the civilian's viewpoint. The next shot allows us to see the soldier fashioning a noose and the angle is such that we know that it is an objective viewer's shot. Further, for a moment during the shot, the soldier's head is framed by the loop, suggesting that Enrico wants us to consider the image as an ironic symbol—all men must die but the soldier is not aware of this. Seen out of context, this shot might be too obviously symbolic and the viewer might think rather than feel; but coming directly after the subjective emotions of the previous shot, Enrico achieves a subtle balance between thought and feeling. We feel with Farquhar, but we are simultaneously allowed to withdraw from his emotional state and think about what we are seeing as well.

During one instance in part two Enrico links us with Farquhar through a series of subjective shots followed by an objective shot, but all employ a moving camera. In shot 18 we (Farquhar) watch the soldiers on the bank through the trestles of the bridge and then turn our head past the trestles and focus upon the lone soldier standing at attention at one end of the bridge. (This is accomplished by a pan and a zoom "track.") The next shot is an objective close-up of Farquhar staring at the soldier's back. Suddenly, he turns his head in the opposite direction. This shot is followed by a zoom "track" towards the back of the soldier standing at attention on the other end of the bridge. The next shot (21—similar to 19) allows us to objectively view Farquhar staring at that soldier, but it continues with the civilian quickly turning his head to crane over his shoulder. We then have a zip diagonal up to the sentinel standing on a hill behind him. Given the camera movement in this last objective shot, we have become emotionally involved in Farquhar's search for a way out of the trap he is in.

In another grouping a few shots later, Enrico employs a different method to allow us to mix our objective view of the action with Farquhar's subjective view. In shot 24 we see the civilian's feet on the springing plank in a close-up objective view. In the next shot we see a piece of driftwood floating downstream and conclude that this is a continued objective view; but the following shot (26) is an objective close-up of Farquhar looking down at the water, supposedly looking at the floating driftwood, and we realize that we have been seeing something from his point of view. The shot concludes with the man looking straight ahead and closing his eyes. Next, we are shown his reason for doing so, we see the sun glaring in the distance.

While this part of the film contains interesting methods used to elicit emotional response, it is relatively objective (twenty-three of thirty-five shots are objective views, only twelve of the thirty-five shots employ a moving camera). Four objective "viewer" shots are particular significant. After the series in which we participate with Farquhar in looking for a way out of the trap (18–21), Enrico cuts to an objective long shot taken from a high angle on the hill overlooking the bridge (23). The camera tracks laterally in the direction of the bridge and tilts down to view the file of soldiers as seen from behind. The angle, distance, and motion of the track (the only lateral track in this section) serves to remind us of the first shots of the film. We are taken away from the action for a time and our sense of distance is renewed. The rhythm of the shots reinforces this feeling: (19–28) 4, 5, 7, 9, *22*, 8, 6, 6, 4, 6. Further, the sense of shot 23 as a visual caesura is reinforced by its placement: shot 22, MCU of the civilian's legs being bound; shot 23, LS (HA) of the scene; shot 24, MCU of the civilian's ankles being bound. The other three particularly significant objective shots all occur within the series that completes this section, shots 34–40. Enrico achieves dramatic impact by editing seven static camera shots together, the greatest number of static camera shots in series in the entire film. This, in itself, serves to create tension. The series begins with two objective shots of the bridge (34 and 35) and concludes with an objective long shot of the falling body (40). Shots 36 and 37 consist of extreme close-ups of the civilian's face and of his hands twisting the ropes behind his back. These are followed by a medium shot of the soldiers and a close-up of their feet performing mechanical military duties. Thus, Enrico climaxes this section with representative shots of the elements that have been at play throughout: our objective distanced view of the proceedings, the military precision of the action carrying out the order, and the frantic responses of the civilian as he struggles to find a way out. The rhythm of the shots is also important for the material that is to come. While it is necessary for Enrico to show us that Farquhar is trapped, he has to give us the irrational feeling that the possibility of escape exists. The longest shot in the series (eighteen seconds) contains the least visible information, the close-up of the quivering face of the civilian. While we are watching, we empathize with Farquhar, but the shot goes on and we become puzzled. When Enrico cuts to the man's hands, he is telling us that this is significant. Here, we feel rather than think. If we were to think, we would realize that we should be seeing a close-up of a fraying rope. Of course, if Enrico were to insert such a shot the film would have been ruined because we would have been given a false lead. (Hitchcock sometimes does this, but a feature-length film can be made more complex and we tend to forget more.) When we see Farquhar fall, we have no concrete reason to believe that he will be saved, but the editing rhythm and shot selection have given us reason to hope.

Parts three and four of the film (41–94 and 95–140) create further complexities with respect to our objective and subjective responses. In real time, this action takes place in Farquhar's mind from the time it takes him to fall the remaining distance of the slack in the rope to the time it takes the rope to grow taut and break his neck. In film time, this action takes nearly seventeen minutes. This part of the film could have been presented from Farquhar's subjective point of view with many more moving camera shots and the content could have been highly emotionalized. Enrico could not have done this for two reasons: first, the irony inherent in the difference between what we see and what Farquhar sees would be lost; secondly, we would guess that we were seeing the workings of a man's mind in the split second before death. While many viewers assume that this is what they are seeing anyway, few are so sure that the ending loses its impact. Enrico's manipulation of our objective and subjective responses creates this desired effect.

Part three encompasses the action from the time Farquhar hits the water (41, subjective shot) to the point at which he finally seems to have escaped the soldiers (94, subjective shot). The director manipulates our responses to the action through his use of editing tempo, camera movement, and point of view. Through his use of these techniques, we not only experience the action from

Farquhar's perspective, we also are distanced somewhat from the action so that we do not feel that we are simply experiencing the civilian's fantasy world. Given the premise of the film, the mind's ability to distort concrete experience for purposes of survival, Enrico had to achieve this ambiguous subjective-objective mix in order to make the film work.

Part three may be divided into three sections, and Enrico employs tempo, movement, and point of view differently in each section. The first section consists of Farquhar's underwater attempts to extricate himself from his bonds and swim back up to the surface. Although he is underwater for about 100 seconds, a long time to hold one's breath considering the energy expended in the physical struggle to get free and swim to the surface, his animalistic shriek for air as he breaks the surface convinces us, at the moment, that this is possible. In other words, Enrico does not make any distinction between real time and film time in this sequence; we are willing to believe that what we see is possible even though the editing tempo is such that we feel that we have been under for a longer period of time. All but two underwater shots are held for eight seconds or less, but shots 47 (twenty-two seconds) and 53 (sixteen seconds) seem interminable within the context of the other shots. The rapid cutting of this sequence, combined with the two relatively lengthy shots, serves to create the needed ambiguity. *Physically*, we are willing to believe that Farquhar is capable of holding his breath for 100 seconds; *psychologically*, the editing tempo leads us to doubt it. The camera movement (all tilts) in this sequence tends to reinforce our psychological reaction. We watch the body drop for thirty seconds of film time (42–46), and the depth of the plunge is further emphasized by the tilting camera. Shot 47, the longest shot in the sequence, is perfectly placed. Farquhar has reached the depth of his plunge and we begin to doubt that he will ever reach the surface. The man seems trapped. Although he struggles, the shot remains static, and it seems to go on and on. The lack of upward movement is emphasized and we begin to respond as frenetically as Farquhar does. As he begins his long struggle to the surface, the camera almost grudgingly tilts upward in a few shots to follow his movement (51 and 54). In shot 55, we reach the surface a brief second before the civilian, and we are rewarded with the sight of the man thrusting his body through the water and shrieking for air. With respect to camera movement, Enrico has manipulated our responses so that we experience the doubt, the struggle, and the exhilaration with Farquhar although the point of view of the shots in this sequence is not subjective. We remain underwater with Farquhar, but we do not experience the action subjectively. Shot 46 begins as though it were subjective, a view of the sunlight glinting on the water overhead, but the camera tilts down to the falling body and we realize that the perspective was objective.

The second section of part three presents the action from the point at which Farquhar looks around after coming to the surface to the shot in which the soldier fires his rifle at him (55–72). He surfaces and looks around; a non-synch, non-local voice sings about a living man and the wonders of nature; we see close-ups of vegetation and insects; the soldiers on the bridge react and make ready to fire; he looks up at the soldiers on the bridge; they look down at him; a soldier fires. While the editing tempo changes throughout this sequence in order to create tension, the difference between this part of the film and the previous sequence is that Enrico makes a distinction through editing between real time and screen time. About two and a quarter minutes of film time elapse from the time Farquhar reaches the surface of the water to the time he is fired upon. In real time, one would suspect that at least one soldier would have immediately spotted him five or ten yards further downstream and would have fired upon him in less than thirty seconds. The director, of course, is aware of our natural response to the action. The emotions we have while we watch the fifty-second sequence of images of nature are a mixture of pleasure and fear. We enjoy the flow of the images and the sound of the music, but we dread the inevitable. We want Farquhar to move; yet, for about two minutes and fifteen seconds, he treads water and looks about.

Viewers are well aware of cinematic conventions that enable the director to expand or compress film time at will; at the very least, they are intuitively aware of such conventions. These conventions have been with us almost since the advent of film. However, Enrico risks pushing the conventions too far in this part of the film, for our concentration upon the central action, Far-quhar's attempted escape, is halted for nearly fifty seconds as we view microscopic scenes of nature. This is a calculated risk on the director's part, for he knows that we will be more inclined to accept blatant expansions of time if it is clear that we are privy to a subjective vision of a character or of the director, himself. In this case, Enrico must lead us to understand that we are seeing reality through Farquhar's eyes. If this is understood, the disjunctive time expansion will be accepted. However, the shots of nature have created a problem for some. Since a number of viewers are unable to willingly suspend disbelief (Farquhar cannot see the images in such close-up detail from his perspective in the middle of the stream), the premise of the plot breaks down for them and they suspect that what they are seeing is only to be found in the mind of the civilian. For them, the building suspense ends when Farquhar comes to the surface and looks around.

Admittedly, Enrico was faced with a crucial problem at this point in the film. He accounted for the time disjunction by switching to a subjective point of view, but he could not allow the film to become wholly subjective from shot 55 onwards or we would be aware that we were merely experiencing the dream of a man totally dedicated to survival. Since the shock of the film is based on the concern that we should not be fully aware of this until the last several shots, the director attempts to resolve this problem in shots 56–62 through a kind of purposeful ambiguity. He wants to give us intimations that what we are seeing is a dream, an imagining, but he does not want us to realize this. Thus, ambiguity is achieved with shots that appear to be Farquhar's subjective views of nature but are clearly beyond his physical capacities. Similarly, the movement of the frame in these shots is created by the zoom lense and this creates ambiguity. While the images are surely lyrical expressions of the wonder and beauty of nature, we realize that the subjectivity of the shots is created by the mechanics of the camera itself and not by Farquhar's vision. Since the theme expressed in these shots, man's heightened appreciation of life in the face of death, is particularly appropriate at this point in the film, Enrico has to risk giving viewers too much information and attempts to cover himself through ambiguity.

Once Enrico has us accept his premises in the nature shots, the remainder of this part of the film follows logically. With the sound of an owl, the director cuts from a close-up of a spider to three shots of the soldiers on the bridge (63–65). Once we assume that the images of nature have been viewed from Farquhar's perspective, Enrico can cut to the bridge seen (roughly) from the civilian's point of view, and we will continue to assume we are seeing what Farquhar sees. This idea is reinforced by the slow-motion movement of the men on the bridge as they see Farquhar and prepare to fire upon him. During these three shots (45 seconds), the camera speed decreases so that by shot 66 the movement is normal again. Here, Enrico covers himself beautifully, for he has implied, through time distortions, that we have experienced what Farquhar has experienced during the last minute and one-half. By shot 66 Farquhar and the viewer have transcended the emotional shock of near-death and have returned to reality as experienced in normal time durations. Because we realize this after the fact of the time-distortion experience, the emotions created by that experience still remain and Enrico can play upon them later in the film to sharpen our sense of ambiguity. Indeed, part of the success of the film is dependent upon the ways in which further instances of ambiguity are created.

From shot 66 to the end of part three, editing tempo is uniformly rapid as Farquhar watches the men on the bridge as they prepare to fire. The civilian seems frozen in place. The camera, correspondingly, is frozen, but movement in the shots is created by the lense as it zooms in to a MCU of the man (66) and reverses the angle and zooms in to a MS of a soldier aiming his rifle. Disconcertingly, Farquhar continues to tread water and stare up at the men on the bridge. The soldier takes aim (69), the angle reverses, and we zoom in to a MCU of Farquhar (70). Then, prior to a MS of the soldier firing the rifle, Enrico cuts to an ECU of the civilian's eye (71). Here, again, we are puzzled. We expect certain normal reactions by Farquhar, but they are not forthcoming. He knows that he is going to be shot at, but he does not attempt to swim away until after the initial rifle shot (73).

The effect of the editing rhythm, the zoom shots, and the reaction shots is that of a kind of ritual out of time. It simply does not ring true. The ECU of Farquhar's eye as he looks at the soldier adds to the unreality of the scene. In the moment before the bullet is fired, the frame is filled with a gigantic eye that may best be seen as a commentary image, but of what? The image of the eye is neutral, we are not sure of its meaning. Perhaps Enrico wants to suggest that the man is immobilized by what he sees and is frozen in the water. Perhaps the eye implies that what we see is in the mind of Farquhar. At any rate, the image reinforces the ambiguity of the scene and further serves to keep us confused about the nature of the action we are viewing.

The remaining action in part three is presented conventionally. That is, Enrico refers back to some of the basic themes and techniques developed in part two. This choice has the effect of bringing us back into the normal world of the story which serves to help us to forget the intended confusions we feel from the time Farquhar hits the water to the time he is fired upon. We see him responding in a normal fashion to the normal world he has created. Farquhar is shot at and he attempts to escape by swimming away from the bridge. The editing tempo is conventional: shots of Farquhar swimming away are inter-cut with shots of the moving soldiers firing upon him. In the beginning of this sequence the shots of Farquhar swimming are held for longer durations than the shots of the soldiers reacting. As Farquhar continues to escape, and as we begin to believe that he will make it, the shots of the soldiers are held for durations roughly equal to the shots of the swimmer. This is a fairly conventional rhythm used to create tension during such an action. The idea expressed is also conventional within the context of the film in that it was developed in part two: the mechanized, unemotional responses of the soldiers to the civilian (76–79). The camera set-ups are further proof of the conventional: although there is a great deal of camera movement in this series of shots (thirteen of twenty-two shots employ movement), the lateral track is the most arresting movement, a good tension-producing technique in this context. Lateral tracks serve to have us see Farquhar's position in the water relative to the soldiers on the bank and vice versa (75, 80, 81, 84, 86). While all of the moving shots in this section reinforce the emotions of the action, the lateral tracks distance us and remind us of similar distancing effects earlier in the film. The point of view in this sequence is also conventional: while we view action from perspectives roughly equal to those of the characters, the perspective is still objective. We see the soldiers on the bank from the water, but when we see Farquhar, he is swimming downstream and looking in that direction; when we see Farquhar from the river bank, the camera position and its movement is not related to any of the soldiers.

Finally, the ambiguity begun in the "nature" sequence of the film continues. Consider the soldiers' arsenal of weapons: the firing of rifles and pistols from the bridge (given the angle and distance, Farquhar is a sitting duck), the unison firing by the file (shot 78 emphasizes the precision of the aiming), and the firing of the cannonball (given the range, Farquhar should have been blown out of the water). As the commanding officer tells the civilian from the bridge, he is trapped; but we accept the escape because we want him to escape. Enrico is counting on this, and he pushes our credibility but not (for most viewers) to the breaking point. Yet, again, we know that something is wrong. Enrico further risks credibility in the shots after the cannonball hits the water. Farquhar sluggishly swims out of the turbulent water and is immediately confronted by a snake coiling through the water towards him (89). He simply dives underwater and swims away from the apparent danger. This kind of cheap serial threat seems out of place in this tightly plotted film and while after we have seen the entire film we might understand the snake as a dream fabrication, the effect in context is disconcerting and keeps us off balance. The section ends with a subjective spinning shot of trees and sky, and we realize that Farquhar has, indeed, escaped.

Enrico continues his basic strategies in part four (95–140). Since three-fourths of the shots contain camera movement, the material is emotionalized; however, only two shots (107 and 125) are presented from Farquhar's point of view. Furthermore, the camera often seems to have a mind of its own, discovering and commenting upon the action. The effect of all of this is very much like the effect of the opening and closing of the film—the viewer responds emotionally but, simultaneously, is distanced from the action. This is exactly what Enrico wants. He wants us to be emotionally involved and he does not want us to really know that we are watching Farquhar's last desperate dream as he plunges to his doom.

Shots 97 and 100 exemplify the discovering camera. In the first shot, the civilian is carried by the river and lost in the white water under a foaming fall. The camera halts its pan, remains static for a moment, quickly pans downriver, and finally discovers the body as it rises out of the water further downstream. Although the camera motion is smooth, its logic is cinéma-verité logic, and this helps to make the action realistic. In the second shot, the camera tracks parallel past a river bank and discovers Farquhar lying in an inlet. The sense of real space around the man leads us to believe that we are viewing an actual happening.

The commenting camera is very evident in this part of the film. Here, again, Enrico gives us intimations of the action as dream, but they are not as jarring as those noted in earlier sections. Shot 109, an ELS (AHA) of the man seen across the river in the distance, is one such intimation. The height and distance from which he is viewed emphasizes his insignificance. The cannon could not reach him, and the soldiers could not know where he was. Yet, a shell explodes nearby, and he runs into the woods. This action makes sense only as an image in a dream. Naturally, Enrico must not give us time to think about this. In shots 110–113, we are bombarded with moving camera images of Farquhar running through the woods. The background and foreground are blurred by short-focus shots, and an up-tempo drumming reinforces the imagery. In short, Enrico offers the intimations and then helps us to forget them. In 114–121, he continues to mix discovering and observing moving camera shots in order to keep us off balance.

This shot sequence modulates into one of the most interesting moments in the film, Farquhar running and walking down a road between two rows of tall trees. Shot 122 begins with a view of a road with geometrically spaced trees receding to form a kind of white triangle against the sky in the lower center of the frame. The white triangle reminds us of the shape of the tent seen in shot 18; the similar shapes suggest the source of one of Farquhar's dream images. At any rate, the white triangle seen behind the man as he begins to run towards us ironically contrasts with the black square seen at the reverse end of the road in 125. In the latter shot, we see where Farquhar is going, and we see him moving toward darkness, his death. Further, the perfectly spaced trees receding in perspective is reminiscent of paintings by de Chirico and Dali. Such images often serve as symbols of time; Enrico's choice of setting is singularly appropriate. Farquhar is attempting to run beyond time.

Shot 122 is the longest in the film (fifty-eight seconds), and its very length serves to reinforce its meaning. Apart from its symbolic significance, the use of the moving commenting camera is quite striking. As Farquhar runs toward the constantly receding tracking camera at full speed, the drumming grows louder and he begins to stagger, struggle, and gasp for breath. He falls, and the camera tilts down to observe him. At this point the camera becomes a commentator rather than an observer. Farquhar lies on the ground, but the camera continues to track and stops about ten yards further on. It's as though the camera is a character and is urging him on. Here, Enrico buttresses our desires by using the camera as our surrogate.

Later, when the camera brushes through the branches of a willow tree, disclosing a view of Farquhar's home, Enrico no longer has need for balance. Reverse angle shots of wife gliding towards husband and husband frantically running towards wife locks us into the tension of the moment and there is not time for thought (131–139). The metronomic regularity of the music that has replaced the "alive" theme is an ominous foreshadowing of what is to come as well as a symbol of time, itself. The dreamlike movement of Abby against the realistic movements of Farquhar, the tracking camera moving in on Abby as she glides forward, the zoom-out pulling Farquhar towards Abby, the short focus as it blurs foreground and background, the editing that forces repetitions of previously completed movements—all of this compresses our fears and hopes into a perfectly controlled ninety seconds of high tension. When the camera stops moving and the music stops (140), we know, in those brief seconds, that we are in a dream.

The silence is ominous; we view the scene over Abby's shoulder. A droning sound; a fall through Abby's arms; a fall out of the bottom of the frame; a dead man with a broken neck dangling from a bridge. Most horribly, the idea of Abby stimulated Farquhar's dream of life, and Abby's dream-touch upon his neck awakens him to death.

In the last brief section of the film (141–144), we are returned to the more objective world of the lateral track. However, unlike the first section of the film, the effect is ironic. We cannot return to the role of objective viewer. The discovering camera has discovered too much. Like Farquhar, we will die.

As suggested earlier, Vidor invites us to *think* about what we are seeing, while Enrico wants us to *respond emotionally*. In "The Bridge," the emphasis is upon the O'Henry ending. Vidor is not as interested in having us believe, for a time, that the civilian escapes the soldiers as he is in having us discover the reason for the hanging written on the poster at the very end of the film. Furthermore, the philosophic implications of mutable man caught in immutable time are of no great concern to Vidor. Thus, the film exists as a trick, a mind game in which the final part of the puzzle falls into place in the last shot. Given this approach to the material, Vidor's static camera and rhythmic editing emphasis is valid. Enrico, on the other hand, is more involved with the philosophic implications of his material. His strategy is akin to those found in Penn's *Bonnie and Clyde* (1967) and Peckinpah's *The Wild Bunch* (1969). All three films are similar in that each director attempts to implicate the viewer in the philosophic premises of the film. In the features, both directors wish to have the viewer respond to the evils of violence by having him see it in himself. In Enrico's film, the director wants the viewer to understand his mutability by seeing it in Farquhar. Enrico wants us to believe, for a time, that Farquhar escapes, but he also wants us to suspect what our eyes see. In this way, the film represents our dreams as well as our realities. Enrico's emphasis upon camera movement, particularly the objective-subjective ambiguity of the lateral track, is a valid cinematic device for achieving that end.

One question remains to be answered: Which approach is more appropriate to the similar content of the two films? In truth, this is an unanswerable question, for the difference in stylistic emphasis creates different content. I prefer the Enrico film because its greater range of concerns is expressed with imagination and technical facility.

SUGGESTIONS FOR PAPERS

Suggestions for Papers

1. In Bierce's short story the reader is aware of the conflict between individual man and his life desire on the one hand, and the detached, impersonal forces that threaten life on the other. Describe how Bierce and Enrico depict these forces and place them in juxtaposition.

2. Woodruff claims that Bierce leads the reader to participate "in the split between imagination and reason, to *feel* that the escape is real while he *knows* that it is not." Does Enrico succeed in leading the viewer to participate in the same manner? Explain.

3. Discuss Farquhar's "escape-journey" in the short story and in the two films. What techniques do Bierce, Vidor, and Enrico use to make the "escape-journey" appear to be real?

4. In part two of the story, Bierce describes Farquhar's life prior to his experience on the bridge. Some critics contend that this background information creates sympathy for the protagonist. Since the filmmakers do not include this information, have they found other successful ways of creating sympathy? Explain.

5. Crane remarks that Farquhar is a man "driven by the need for his family." Is this a convincing explanation of the protagonist's motivation? How do Bierce, Vidor, and Enrico treat the relationship between Farquhar and his family?

6. To what extent do the short story and the two film adaptations reflect a pessimistic and cynical view of the world and a damning indictment of war?

7. Critics of both the short story and the Enrico adaptation object to what they see as "sentimentality" and "melodrama." Consult a dictionary of literary terms, define the two terms, and determine the validity of the charges. Offer specific details to support your views.

8. Select a fictional element (character, point of view, imagery, etc.) in Bierce's story and suggest how Enrico adapts this element to film. How would you describe the nature of the adaptation? How would you evaluate it?

9. Bierce's story may be said to be concerned with the conflict of mutable man living in immutable time. Many film theorists believe that film is better able than literature to present this sense of man vs. time due to the nature of the medium. For example, in *Film: The Creative Process*, John Howard Lawson notes that "film alone can weave a time pattern in which all the parts are equally vivid." Given this view, do the filmmakers tend to play to their strength by emphasizing the theme of time in their respective films? Does time seem more vivid in the films than it does in the short story? Explain.

10. In Nicola Chiaromonte's "On Image and Word" (*Encounter*, Jan. 1963), the point is made that "the cinematic image can support interpretations that are absolutely contradictory." Present evidence from the Shadoian and Bellone essays that tends to support this view. Do you find similar evidence of contradictory interpretations of the short story that could be based on a thesis about the nature of language and would resemble Chiaromonte's comment on the nature of the cinematic image? What conclusions are you able to draw from all of this?

11. Chiaromonte also calls the reader's attention to a cinematic fallacy: "the assumption that complex emotions and subtle ideas, which can be expressed *adequately only in language* can be rendered in *moving photographs.*" Give some examples from the essays on the story in which the critics allude to the nature of the emotions and ideas in Bierce's work and hypothesize Shadoian's as well as Bellone's reactions to these examples with respect to their judgment of the success of the film adaptation.

12. Describe, as clearly as possible, how Enrico transforms the literary strengths of the story into cinematic strengths.

13. Making use of the materials in this book and your viewing of the films, construct Vidor's and Enrico's theories of film adaptations. Do their theories differ significantly? Explain.

14. Both Vidor and Enrico have chosen to eliminate certain passages and ideas that are in the story, while each adds some material of his own to the film. Account for these decisions.

15. Describe Vidor's and Enrico's interpretations of the short story. Do the director's interpretations differ significantly? Which of the story's critics share their respective views?

16. Are the films successful adaptations of the short story? Does one seem more successful than the other? Explain.